MW01122423

RISJ CHALL~~~~~

Why Documentaries Matter

Nick Fraser

REUTERS
INSTITUTE for the
STUDY of
JOURNALISM

Reality is providence.
Al Maysles

But they never said how beautiful it was.
George Orwell on reading the reviews of *Animal Farm*

The most important modern philosophical problem is attention.
Simone Weil

Contents

Executive Summary

In appearance the survival of documentaries would not appear to be an urgent topic. They are a staple of broadcast programming, relied on by public broadcasters to secure audiences, and restricted in their formal ambitions. No argument exists publicly about how they should be funded and indeed whether their existence is threatened. But this is far from being the case. Documentaries exist precariously, for the most part under-funded and often neglected by broadcasters. Worldwide the budgets for documentaries are falling. Their creators live a hand-to-mouth existence. But documentaries must also be classed among the remarkable, culturally innovative forms of our time. In the last 20-odd years they have come into their own. They are revered by critics, and celebrities queue to attach their names. Globally, many festivals exist to promote documentary. Some documentaries, though not many, have made substantial profits at the box office.

Do documentaries matter? Why do they matter? They do, certainly, but in order to demonstrate their worth it is necessary to revisit their origins. After a first frisson of interest in the capability of film to depict real life, they became poor relations of contemporary fictions. Documentaries subsisted for a long time on state patronage, with very mixed results. A heyday of sorts ensured their survival within busy television schedules. But truly innovative films have been made when funding has been available from a mixture of sources – from television, film funds, private investors, foundations. Nowadays, with the arrival of the internet as a means of distribution, the prospects of documentaries seem bright. But documentaries are threatened, too, by the decline of television funding.

In this 'Challenge' I argue for the recognition that documentaries are a public good, comparable (in this respect and in others) to serious reporting. They have become one of the means by which we connect to the contemporary world, making sense of it. They do occupy an important place in contemporary media culture, not just in Europe and North America but globally. Something called documentary will survive any mutations in distribution or perceptions of culture caused by the internet. But good and valuable films will flourish only if we pay more attention to their funding. What is needed is not any radical rethinking of the documentary form, or indeed any alteration in the way films are funded. Instead, in a series of what social psychologists call 'nudges', we need to readdress each of the different things that go to ensure not just the creation of a film but its wide and successful distribution globally. In the last chapter I itemise some 'nudges'.

Foreword

This is an argument in favour of documentaries. Think of them taxonomically, not as a tribe, but a vast assemblage of variegated fowls or mammals constituting a species whose continued existence everyone finds hard to explain. They're among the least valued, and most interesting, cultural forms of our time. Improbably, however, they have emerged from a cave of unknowing into something like sunlight, enjoying a certain vogue. Greater things are expected of them, as if they had somehow displaced print journalism in our efforts to understand things; and they are now being sold as a means to save the world. I am in part sympathetic to such ambitions, and I regard the current success of documentaries as no more than a recognition belatedly afforded to them.

Nonetheless, the much-hailed triumph of documentary films subsists on the shakiest of foundations. After many years, shoulder to the wheel, I am concerned at the increasing difficulty in funding them. Why are most people who make documentaries, even by the appalling standards of freelance journalism, so poor? Can documentaries be funded as books and print are, by the market? Will they be assisted by new possibilities of payment made possible by the internet? Are the economics of documentaries so hopelessly skewed that this isn't an option? Should they continue to rely on television, with which they enjoy a relationship best characterised as a long, intermittently satisfactory, marriage of convenience, in which both partners grumblingly submit, with occasional, overwhelmingly unsuccessful, attempts to change things, or even attempts to get free, dissolving the union? Are documentaries a definitively niche form? Should they be thought of as campaigning tools, as just one aspect of the many efforts to improve the world? Do they really change anything?

Among the relatively small number of people whose job it is to commission documentaries and the larger group who make them, often under forbidding circumstances, such questions are hotly debated. My own conclusions are that documentaries are attractive, sturdy hybrids, capable of survival in adverse circumstances. They do many things for us, most of them good. They will benefit best not by systematised assistance, but by our ability to calculate or guess, with a degree of approximation, what is best for them. We can best do that if we think about how they work for us.

1.   Yes, Documentaries Matter

Documentaries began as a casual experiment in seeing what happened when you pointed a camera at the things around you. They never caught on in cinemas, and were displaced by fiction. For a long time the genre was kept alive by a mixture of corporate and government patronage, with mixed results. Broadcast television saved the form, supplying documentaries with a steady supply of funds and enabling films to reach large audiences. Recently, however, broadcasters have appeared to tire of documentaries. They are shown in cinemas, with fitful results, and they are beginning to carve out a place online. The partial liberation of documentaries from television has enabled film-makers to produce a great number of brilliant films, to the degree that it may now be said that the documentary has finally become a recognisable cultural form. But so much success hasn't resolved the precarious nature of documentary film, far from it; and film-makers still struggle to make good work.

Nowadays it's common to hear documentary film described as the new rock and roll. It was a documentary that saved Al Gore from political oblivion, winning him an Oscar. Few Hollywood directors have actually made documentaries (Scorsese is an exception, though Werner Herzog has been able once again to make fictions as a consequence of his successful documentaries) but it has become commonplace to see the names of Brad Pitt, Leonardo di Caprio, or Sam Mendes attached to films as executive producers. Patrons such as the Ford Foundation, George Soros, Robert Redford's Sundance Institute, Gucci, and Puma lend their blessing, giving funds to film-makers. And in 2010 Oprah Winfrey bestowed her own special benediction on the documentary form at Sundance, pledging to do for it what she had done for books by creating a documentary club on her brand-new cable channel OWN.

Among film festivals, Sundance occupies a special place. It's keenly cutting edge, a bit recherché, and it has a record of having been right about the direction taken by film culture. People will keep you abreast of gossip at Sundance, and that tends to be focused on the deals being done that lift the odd film from obscurity to success. But another preoccupation has crept into the Sundance scene. People talk about documentary films now. They don't tend to say how much money these films are about to make. Instead they tell each other how good the docs are, how much better indeed than the fictional offerings. Films that only a few years ago would have been restricted to the smallest audiences are now packed out. They're received rapturously, and audiences are reluctant to let their makers leave the Q and A sessions afterwards.

I've watched documentary films on behalf of my own patron and employer the BBC. I've reached the point where I can no longer recall how many thousands of films I have seen. The irony is that for a long time I didn't really like documentaries. I had an omnivorous interest in different forms of reportage; specifically, I was interested in the ways in which reporters, while retaining a degree of objectivity, might shift public opinion. But I found many documentaries to be staid and predictable, overliteral in their approach and hobbled by an often unacknowledged left-wing bias. I became interested in them out of a hunch: that they were about to become important, and that I should try and stake some sort of claim in a new field.

On arrival in the BBC, in 1995, I was sent *Hoop Dreams*, a recently completed film chronicling five years in the lives of two black inner-city teenagers who wished to become basketball stars. The film was more than two hours and forty minutes long, and the first time I sat down to watch it, I was interrupted after ten minutes. Luckily I persevered. As I had been told, the quality of the images improved after seventeen minutes, when the film-makers began to use a more up-to-date camera. But the story of William Gates and Arthur Agee was engulfing. After an hour you felt that knew them, and you knew all about the Chicago school system after an hour and a half. It was possible to think of *Hoop Dreams* as something new. In the 1960s, Norman Mailer began to refer to something called the 'non-fiction novel' in which the lives of real characters could be displayed in the sort of depth that one might associate with fiction. Although there were many series or long-form films depicting individuals or communities,[1] no one as yet had attempted quite the same thing in the medium of film. In this respect, *Hoop Dreams* was a pioneering work, and an impressive one.

In 2011 one of the directors of *Hoop Dreams* was back at Sundance with *The Interrupters*, a two-and-a-half-hour account of the battles against violence waged by social workers on Chicago's South Side. The film's premise was simple: violence was a plague. It could never be eradicated unless its root

---

1   Mailer's masterpiece, *The Executioner's Song*, is 1,000-odd pages of meticulously edited documentary transcript, and many docs, not least *When We Were Kings* (1996), are graced by his presence. In Britain, such works as Michael Apted's *7 Up* series (1964 onwards), Paul Watson's *The Family* (1974), Molly Dineen's *The Ark* (1993), and Phil Agland's *Beyond the Clouds* (1994) are instances of long-form series in which the lives of so-called ordinary people receive intensive, often passionate attention. The vast œuvre of Fred Wiseman is another example. But these films don't display the qualities of plotting to be found in *Hoop Dreams*, nor do they focus so intensively, in the style of novelists, on the emergence of character through incident.

causes – decades of underemployment, a macho culture, drugs, etc. – were eliminated, and that wasn't going to happen, not for decades anyhow. But it was possible to contain and even arrest the spread of violence. You did this by entering the gangs, persuading each of the members that they would die unless they, too, fought against the plague. Former gang members, often those who had spent time in prison on drug charges or even for murder, formed a cadre of specialists, dressed in a red livery and speaking in street idiom. Steve James followed them as they went about their task, comforting the many bereaved families of murdered teenagers, urging gang members to desist.

I was struck, too, by something else – how used to watching long films the audience had become, and how easily accepted was the slang of the South Side. There was nothing staid or unoriginal about *The Interrupters*. But the passionate applause showed how, courtesy of fictions such as *The Wire*, which were themselves heavily influenced, even dominated by the documentary tradition, with their shaky cameras, their discontinuities, and crusading naming names style, films like The *Interrupters* were part of a mainstream now. This was another marker in the wide, general acceptance of ambitious, well-made documentaries.[2]

'Documentary,' says the dictionary: 'Noun. Based on or recreating an actual event, era, life story, that purports to be factually accurate and contains no fictional elements.' This is useful, so far as it goes, but excessively minimal. Why shouldn't non-fiction contain elements of fiction? And why should something only 'purport' to be factually accurate? When you describe anything, it is altered. The act of seeing plainly modifies what is seen. It isn't necessary to be a visionary to understand this. Plainly, too, the photographic recording of actuality complicates things. I am a camera, Christopher Isherwood's famous formulation from 1930s Berlin, isn't in the least convincing. We may own or use photographic means of reproduction; however, we don't and cannot become cameras. But the discussion of documentaries has been dogged, perhaps understandably, by photographic literalism.

In a late, elegiac poem, Robert Lowell comes closest to recreating the act of description:

> *Yet why not say what happened?*
> *Pray for the grace of accuracy*
> *Vermeer gave to the sun's illumination*
> *Stealing like the tide across a map*
> *To his girl solid with yearning.*
> *We are poor passing facts,*

2   *Hoop Dreams* was never nominated for an Oscar. *The Interrupters*, to the astonishment of people who make and talk about documentaries, failed even to make the short list of films compiled each year by the committee appointed by the Academy.

Warned by that to give
Each figure in the photograph
His living name.

Lowell died a year after writing this poem, in the back of a New York taxi, clutching a Lucian Freud portrait of his estranged girlfriend. He was only 59, and his life had been marred by the grotesque deformations of reality caused by a severe bipolar affliction. I like these sad end-of-life lines because they show that there's no real conflict between the desire for accuracy, and the spirit of illumination. You might think ('poor passing facts') that saying exactly what happened is a lowly, banal activity. No, Lowell is saying, it isn't, it's far from being banal. Indeed it is so important that one must pray for it. It does represent a kind of grace, though not of course in any religious sense. But there is no single reliable way of capturing anything, as a second, more careful reading of the poem reveals. The sun steals across our lives. We map its course – but how do we ever know how this is done? (As Lowell's sudden end reveals, we will never wholly know when we are done.) We might of course conclude that there is some Zen-like secret implied by the art of observing things. In reality, we are changed by the act of observation, as well as the objects and people on which we try to focus. We cannot rely on anything, let alone sight, or any machine as fallible as a camera. Most likely, we will resolve to hope for the best, repudiating both literalism and the excess use of metaphors. At the very least 'documentation' requires a copious supply of guile and stealth combined with the sort of exactitude, to use only one, easily replaceable example, that allows one to single out a Cartier Bresson photograph at any reasonable distance. Let's be honest, drudgery is part of it, and rote, as well as obsessiveness. But nothing, as Lowell insists, should rightly be excluded. How else will the names come alive?

Documentaries do have their enemies, conscious or inadvertent, and I can anticipate a degree of opposition to these claims. Why fret about the future of a lowly form, widely considered to be on a par with the other offerings of television? Why attempt to elevate what is no more than the cunning assembly of sound and images into more or less plausible narratives? Documentaries, it will be said, have for a long time occupied a humble position in the television economy, securing audiences reliably for a relatively low cost. Many people, year after year, have been comforted by the experience of watching slices of life carved out of familiar material for their distraction. There is no need, surely, to investigate their relationship with reality. My reply to such observations is that the widespread uncritical acceptance of documentaries did damage their prospects. A cultural snobbery still surrounds documentaries. They've been regarded as filler primarily, alternatively as a form of agitprop – and they are still condescended to, by journalists (though less so recently) and film critics, even by those who make documentaries.[3]

Do documentaries matter? Why do they matter? Unless they matter to us, it is hard to see why they should continue to receive public subsidy. This is a large question, easily posed and hard to answer. I believe they do matter. Before saying why this is the case, however, it seems appropriate to detail some of the ways in which they have been undermined, both by their successes and their failures.

Take, first, an extreme example of the degree to which the depiction of reality in film was prejudiced by its associations with the state. In 1997 I went to St Petersburg in order to work with the film-maker Viktor Kossakovsky on *Wednesday*, a film in which he rendered in counterpoint the day of his own birth, 19 July 1961, with the lives of others born on the same day in the city that was then part of the Soviet Union, and known as Leningrad. Under Communism, everyone was supposed to be equal and therefore enjoy a similar life, and Viktor's efforts were directed to demonstrating how the contrary had happened. A few of those he found had indeed got rich, but most were poor, some indeed alcoholics or drug addicts, and the film showed signs of slipping into a contemporary description of the St Petersburg's lower depths. We needed to show what had been dreamed of in the days of identical ambitions, egalitarian cribs, and Pioneer rallies. So Viktor and I went to Lenfilm, the old Communist archives located in a crumbling Stalinist-era building still decorated with plaques in red and dirty white, and watched archive films for a day. We found footage of identical white beds in which small, newly arrived Soviet citizens nestled silently. We also saw samples of lavishly produced weekly accounts of life in which nothing significant happened. The big event was a visit of a surprisingly svelte Fidel Castro, or Nikita Khrushchev's bulky form sighted in a Ukrainian dairy farm. And it was in this respect that our visit proved to be revealing – as a revelation of how much that was filmed, recorded, known as documentaries, was in fact wholly impersonal, dictated by forgotten needs, laid down to plan. There was no idea of any independently acquired truth here, no sense that one could go out with a camera, as one might bearing a pad and a pencil, and simply describe what was happening. Everything was prearranged, controlled from the top.

A milder form of such attitudes was pervasive among broadcasters in the West. They were obliged to serve mass audiences, and it became part of the

---

3   Take one conspicuous instance. Writing in *The New Yorker* (19 Mar. 2012), Richard Brody correctly judges Claude Lanzmann's *Shoah* to be 'among the most distinguished works of art to come out of the late twentieth century'. But he also takes seriously Lanzmann's suggestion that the film 'defies the categories of documentary or fiction'. In his autobiography *The Hare of Patagonia* (Atlantic Books, 2012), 518, Lanzmann calls *Shoah* 'a fiction of the real'. The phrase can be applied, too, to most well-shaped documentary films in which real-life characters attain the vividness of fictional equivalents. Lanzmann's film would be less overpowering as well as less convincing if it had been made as a fiction, with a script and actors, and wasn't literally truthful. The quality of literalness makes it a documentary.

job of television executives to vet product, ensuring its acceptability. Many bland series were made as a consequence of such obligations. Lifeboats were recurrent subjects, as well as vet surgeries. It would be futile as well as snobbish to dismiss such artefacts, because they gave many people much pleasure. Who knows, they probably still convey, however faintly, the idea that we are all humans, sharing the same camera movements, speaking lethargically and in short, easily grasped phrases.

In response to such actions, and as a revolt against mass culture, experimental films came to be highly prized. Documentaries, too, it was thought, must follow the route of experimentation. Briefly, in the 1970s and 1980s, it became fashionable within academies to speak of the death of the author. Critics, viewers or readers, writers, and directors were merely rummaging around in pre-existing artefacts or habits in a quest to update them. Was it possible to be original? Could one even purport to tell the truth? Observers of the cultural scene would reply with a shrug or a nod, implying that the question was a stupid one. Forget about individuals, they said, in one dogmatic article after another. Forget about individuals. All that matters is the pattern in the carpet.

Postmodernism is mercifully out of fashion now, restricted to a few outer reaches of academic culture, but among film critics the view that documentaries do or should resemble narrative fictions remains bizarrely widespread. A recent crop of films mixing fact with fiction prompted these thoughts from Nigel Andrews, film critic of the *Financial Times*:

> *Think about it. Do we still buy, if we ever did, the notion*
> *that non-fiction on-screen is anything other than an artefact?*
> *That it is not shot through with point-of-view, with the*
> *cultural perspectives and prejudices of the day? That it is*
> *not as storied and subjective, in its way, as a narrative*
> *feature film?*[4]

In the *Guardian* Stella Bruzzi, author of *New Documentary*, similarly applauds films 'that are all about the fluctuation between what's staged and what's real'.[5] She thinks that audiences can learn to watch films for their capacity to play with our ideas of the truth.

I am against this aesthetic position, firmly on the side of those making peak-time hedgehog epics. Capturing any sort of reality isn't an ignoble aim. Mixing fact and fiction is a cliché beloved of film aesthetes and Hollywood producers as well as an empty marketing strategy. It has become routine for fictional narratives to claim to be 'real'. How many mainstream Hollywood

4   *Financial Times*, 30 Dec. 2010.
5   *Guardian*, 30 Sept. 2010.

films each year pay homage to the conventions of documentary film? Any representation of reality, in any medium, can reasonably be described as an artefact. But that doesn't mean that all representations are false, or that the ability to distinguish between fact and fiction isn't important.

But why are documentaries not always taken seriously when it comes to giving an account of the world? Among British journalists, themselves seasoned practitioners of the fictionalisation of reality, documentaries were for many years regarded with deep suspicion. It was alleged that most documentaries were faked – those who made them decided on the story, and went out and filmed what they needed. Often the belief that documentaries were fictional coincided with an intense attraction to them. In *The Kindness of Women*, one of his autobiographical volumes, J. G. Ballard describes a 1960s visit to a Copacabana festival of 'scientific and documentary films'. Ballard is excited by the films that will never 'reach the general public': bizarre footage of stress fractures of ice hockey players, split septums, but most of all, as one would expect from the author of *Crash,* the sexual imagery used to desensitise habitual sex offenders:

> *The audience… gazed at the screen with the same steady eyes and the unflinching gaze of the men in the Soho porn theatres or the fans of certain types of apocalyptic science fiction. Whenever the criminal subjects winced with pain or vomited into their sick basins, ripples of appreciation would move across the audience at some particularly striking camera angle or expository close-up as the Soho patrons might have applauded a telling crotch shot or elegant anal penetration.*[6]

In Ballard's novel *The Day of Creation*, French film-makers come to Africa in order to make a 'bogus documentary' about the reclamation of Eden from the desert. When the project they wish to film gets out of hand, defying their expectations, they are swept along in the chaos, caught up in violence. They never finish their film.

The irony is that J. G. Ballard believed in literal, unassailable truth. He also thought that documentaries represented an unrivalled way of depicting reality. Perverse and wonderfully attached to normality, he was, as one might expect, an aficionado of lenses, light meters, obsessively interested in the details of filming. He also thought that, given the chance, human beings would bend any new means of communications to their will, turning truth-telling capabilities into convenient lies. But it is surely significant that Ballard's masterpiece *Empire of the Sun* is constructed like a documentary: rough at the

---

6   J. G. Ballard, *The Kindness of Women* (Harper Perennial, 1991), 240–1.

surface, with many shifts of tone and abruptly memorable set pieces depicting young hero Jim's mysterious ability to grow up, despite hunger, the failings of adults, and the horror of the camp in which he finds himself. One can read the book as a version of a film that Ballard might have wished himself make, and of course never could do. But we know now that such films can be made. Indeed they are made, not every day, perhaps, but certainly every year.

Nonetheless the notion that documentaries are somehow inauthentic lives on. I've encountered it many times. The writer Toby Young once pitched an idea to me of a fake documentary, centred around the efforts of a film-maker to uncover a conspiracy capable of explaining the world. In particular he wanted to capture the moody intensity of film-makers. Journalists had acquired a less sombre, more self-mocking view of their calling. If you worked for a newspaper, you couldn't retain so great a sense of your importance, and you would certainly know how to tell lies. Besides, Toby suggested, no one watched documentaries. Why then were documentary film-makers so obsessed with what they did? Why did they sound like mendicant friars, dolefully tolling bells to warn us of their presence?

Film-makers themselves are by and large unable to shed much light on this enduring mystery. They're concerned with the hows of their trade – practical things like access, visas, lenses, and suchlike. (Light used to be a staple of their discourse, but following the invention of light-adaptable autofocusing cameras, this has fallen off the agenda.) They may talk about why they were attracted to certain narratives. But they are reluctant to say why one set of circumstances rather than another might make for a better, more involving, more lasting film. For a long time, pressed to explain the impact of their films, film-makers would reply in the idiom of John Grierson, founding father of British documentary. Grierson, in his left-wing Calvinist way, believed that films should supply uplift through their capability to depict good lives, or at least lives in which people strove for humanity, and into which the rest of us could enter, thus seeing our sense of ourselves, as democrats and human beings, significantly enlarged by the experience. Viewing such singular, ordinary lives, audiences would experience a degree of solidarity. Many documentaries, to be sure, must have fulfilled this function, though it remains impossible to say how so many individual encounters with reality could have added up to something more significant. Nowadays, with so many channels, and the reluctance of television executives to admit to any large-scale educative function of the medium, the idea of the documentary as a binding force in society, viewed by large number of people and attesting to cultural solidarity, is in decline. It has been replaced, to be sure, by the idea that documentaries can be linked to campaigns and made to change the world. Is this more than a pious hope? On occasions, perhaps they can and do have such effects; but no evidence exists to suggest that film on its own is specially good at social mobilisation. Nor is it evident that film-makers will be well-served by seeing their films bundled into social movements and made to serve the interests of NGOs. This is a newly fashionable idea deemed suitable for an age in which many people believe that the world, unless fixed rapidly, will come to grief. But it is based on an illusion almost as old as documentary film. It is a fact, certainly, that upwards of 40 million people watched *Kony 2012*, a film about an African mass murderer. They argued about the merits of the film afterwards. But it seems unlikely that the film, by itself, amounted to any significant alteration in the way we think. In that sense the Kony film must be seen as part of the activist toolbox. It is a work of liberal propaganda, and like all propaganda should be judged on its effects, and not for what it is.[7]

Continuous transformation of media has become what any world citizen must now expect. Among so many inventions, however, some things don't easily change. When Ted Turner instituted 24-hour satellite news, spreading his network globally, he (and others) imagined that this might be a means whereby people might more easily enter each others' lives. But Turner's dream hasn't endured. The horizons of world news have shrunk, even as powerful governments have created their own news services.[8] Seeking wisdom, or more simply trying to keep up, one can get stuck somewhere between the cacophony of the internet and such officially sponsored views. And it is in this context that documentaries reveal their true utility. It's possible to see what others think. One can even begin to comprehend others, or at least acquire the illusion that this might be possible. This was what the inventor of broadcast journalism Ed Murrow, famously, hoped would become the function of network television – to reveal the existence of sheer difference. It didn't happen that way, of course, but from the periphery, through pinpoints and small actions, documentary films do just that.

In the end all non-fiction may be dissolved online into the generic, undifferentiated category of content, becoming part of an endless, unexaminable chain of media cause and effect. We may not be able to distinguish one statement from another, in much the same way as we now no longer quite know where prose ends and pictures begin, or indeed where the boundary between the instant past and the already future can be drawn. For the moment, however, we can agree that narratives do exist, and that some are more truthful than others. And it is in this space that the best documentaries

---

7   *Guardian*, 14–15 Mar. 2012.
8   CNN, Turner's creation, is less ambitious now, though its non-US service supplies global news with a strong American slant. BBC World News remains hobbled by lack of funds. Al-Jazeera, paid for by the Emir of Qatar, but relatively independent, covers many African and Asian stories neglected in the West. To its credit, it has become the voice of progressive Arab nationalism, giving airtime to democrats throughout the Middle East. Many programmes of Russia Today, however, would not have seemed out of place in Soviet times, and the same is true of China's global services. France 24 occupies an uneasy space between modern, global reporting and the traditional French desire to export cultural values.

exist. I was attracted to docs because I liked them. I still do and I also like the fact that no serious body of theory exists to legitimate them. They have come to subsist, precariously, at a crossroads of contemporary culture, somewhere between journalism, film narrative, and television entertainment. They appear to thrive on contradictions, between the stubborn reality they purport to capture and their necessarily limited means, between the impositions of story-telling and the desire, periodically, to interpret or analyse. They aren't fictional, ever, but they can seem in their attractiveness more real than reality. Ultimately, they remain provisional, snapshot-like; and it helps that they cannot be collected, and are thus immune to the unwelcome attentions of connoisseurs. In fact they appear to be doomed to remain on or outside the perimeters of the culture world, which accounts both for their freshness, and the relative poverty of those who make them.

It is this special, not elsewhere found, quality of being both at the edge and centre of things that makes them matter most of all. They can seem to evoke what the evolutionary biologist Stephen Pinker refers to as 'the widening circle of human sympathy'. They can even, in their insistence that the world is unfathomably plural, let us see humans as individuals. And they accomplish this superlatively, not as a matter of routine but because their makers have taken great care to allow us to share this vision. Claude Lanzmann spent years tracking down Abraham Bomba, the barber who cut the hair of those about to die in Treblinka. In order to bring Bomba's experience to life, Lanzmann made him pretend to cut a friend's hair in a Tel Aviv barber shop. None but a pedant would begrudge this stratagem, or fail to recognise the scene for what it is, a moment that vindicates the notion of filmed reality. But such moments, it must be insisted, are far from rare. They occur in many good documentaries. And they are what we remember of films years afterwards. Just this week, for instance, I watched a scene in which a young Albino in Tanzania, dressed incongruously in a suit and standing in the shade, spoke to an assembly of villagers. Albino body parts were valued for their curative functions, and a horrifying series of murders had occurred. It wasn't safe for Albinos to travel alone, even in daylight. Our protagonist felt he had to tell the villagers that Albinos such as himself were humans, too, and should not be killed. First curious, then attentive, the villagers ended by agreeing with him. I don't think I will easily forget this moment. And I hope it will gain in life as it is viewed, recontextualised, comprehended, and maybe even treasured. This is why documentaries matter.

No one should claim to say what a documentary is or should be. It doesn't seem right to wish to fence in the form, excluding the force fields – dramatic fictions, news, agitprop – that surround it. Nonetheless here are some graffiti-style ways of characterising the good ones.

First, documentaries should be provisional. You shouldn't know where you are going when you start. Second, somewhere – not in a script, perhaps, or by means of a reportorial presence, but through editing, via the lens, or in a barely paraphrasable way, through what they *are* – there must be some notion of an author, or at least that the film was guided by an individual hand, or an association of individually motivated hands. Third, they must represent some sort of creative collision – not with reality, because that's a foolish idea, but with the idea of how anything can or should be depicted. Also, and this is rare, they should be occasionally funny. Most documentaries aren't funny. This is a mistake because the shock of the real isn't without its own humorous aspects.

Last, and most important, those who watch documentaries as well as those who make them should realise that anything goes. There are traditions of film-making, to be sure. But the vitality of the documentary resides in the fact that it thrives at a series of crossroads scarred by accidents. You can arrive at the idea of documentary through tabloid journalism or philosophy, out of a desire to change the world, or merely because there is a story you wish to tell. All you really have to want to do is say what happened.

In his magisterially inclusive compendium of the contemporary cultural scene, *Cultural Amnesia* (2007), Clive James makes the point that never, for those only moderately ingenious, has it been easier to access the totality of world culture. You don't need much money to find out about things. What James has to say is mainly about pictures or words, but it applies even more to information. It is easier these days to know something about fellow inhabitants of the planet. If we so desire, we can understand many more things. This remains the simplest definition of why documentaries matter, and we should ensure that, against the odds, not just great ones but good ones continue to be created and shown throughout the world.

Let me suggest one last reason why we should cherish documentaries. Of the current manifestations of contemporary culture which would you choose to conserve? Thought of as an app, documentaries wouldn't make it. They have no real cultural recognition. They're always seen as part of something else – film, television, journalism, even real life. They inhabit, creatively, a nowhereness, always somewhere between other things; but that turns out to be a very good place from which to observe the contradictions of our times. They may be hard to find, but you would miss them if they went. You might even miss them very much. I've watched documentaries in editing rooms, at festivals, in the endless versions they go through, with so much pain taken and given, before they're finished. I like to watch them with audiences, and at home, too. No one will ever be able to tell me definitively what a documentary does, or how it affects people, any more than we can say for sure what is the cumulative effect of a newspaper report, a sonnet, a Shakespeare tragedy, *Madame Bovary,* or *Mein Kampf.* But I do know that documentaries, taken as individuals, resemble a group of friends. I'd miss them if they went. If the species became extinct, I am convinced that this would be a more than small loss for humanity.

2.   Starting Fires

The first documentary depicted Thomas Edison's assistant pretending to sneeze. Early contributions from the Lumière brothers reveal the movement of waves, brick dust hanging in the air, crowds and workers leaving factories, glaring at the camera. 'The films were not an illusion, or a performance but a grey, flickering reality of a past reality,' Kevin Macdonald and Mark Cousins inform us. 'The cinema, unlike any previous art form, was able to represent the spontaneous – the very essence of life itself.'[9] Early documentaries were popular with audiences, but the novelty of being able to see what happened wore off once fiction films adopted more sophisticated techniques. So began the long struggle of documentary to find its place in the sun. Was it, as its proponents desired, a new form capable of great originality, destined to compete with manufactured cinematic artifice? Or was it filler for harassed exhibitors who required the odd loss leader, or, more discouragingly, something to show before the main feature?

For a long time, the slow development of technology appeared to condemn documentaries to the margins, as did the sheer problem of getting them distributed. Fits and starts characterise documentary history. There is a sense that their protagonists are similarly afflicted – by the passion to describe things, to be sure, but also by a need to work against the grain, creating work in the most improbable circumstances.

Just as significant, however, is the degree to which both the subject matter of documentaries and a degree of formal experimentation were established early on. War footage was much in demand, and much of it was faked for the benefit of early newsreels. The enhancement of reality, it was apparent early on, would be a staple of the new form – not because reality was invariably dull, but because audiences were habituated to dramatic refinements. The most commercially successful early documentary was *With Lawrence of*

---

9   *Imagining Reality: The Faber Book of Documentary* (Faber & Faber, 2006) assembles a selection of writings interspersed with intelligent commentary from two authors with experience of making films. Bizarrely, no comprehensive history of documentary film exists.

Arabia (1920). This was assembled from mostly staged footage shot by the American lecturer and cultural entrepreneur Lowell Thomas. Lawrence was a minor figure until his exploits, as recorded by Thomas, gave him cult status. To begin with, Thomas had hoped to interest audiences in the footage he had accumulated of General Allenby conquering the Holy Land, but this was not to be the case. The audiences wanted Lawrence. They wanted a simple story of heroism that might in part compensate for so much hard to comprehend, apparently meaningless carnage. At the Royal Opera House in Covent Garden, Thomas addressed the royal family, Lloyd George, and Winston Churchill, and even, on one occasion Lawrence himself. 'I saw your show last night,' he wrote to Thomas. 'And thank God the lights were out.'[10]

More typical of the fate of documentaries was the debut of *Nanook of the North* (1922), Robert Flaherty's pop anthropology rendering of Inuit life. Flaherty took his own developing room on location, and he showed footage to the Inuits, provoking a response somewhere between curiosity and rapture. Back in New York exhibitors were less enamoured. The film came out to mixed notices. It played better in London, Paris, and Rome, where it was shown in arthouse cinemas. In his account of the fate of the film Flaherty sounds a wistful, half-defensive tone wholly characteristic of those who try to get documentaries shown to wide audiences. 'You ask me what I think the film can do to make large audiences feel intimate with these distant peoples,' he said. 'Well, *Nanook* is an instance of this. People who read books on the North are, after all, not many, but millions of people have seen this film in the last twenty-six years – it has gone round the world.' When Nanook died of starvation, Flaherty noted, his death was recorded everywhere, 'even in China.'[11] For the rest of his career, Flaherty trod a path wholly familiar to generations of documentary makers. He needed money to make his films, and this often involved promising more than he could deliver. At their best, like *Man of Aran*, Flaherty films deliver powerful narrative. But they cannot be taken seriously as social documents. They belong to the history of documentary.[12]

The rise of documentary proved to be haphazard. Film-makers in search of the means to record reality, it became clear, would have to find sources of patronage outside the increasingly profit-oriented, formula-bound system of film production centred in Hollywood. In the absence of private investors, they turned to the other major contemporary source of funding, the twentieth-century state. Here they found ready backers, but they were required to sign up to the ideologies of the time. Not all cultural bureaucrats were philistines, and

---

10   Ibid. 36.
11   Ibid. 42.
12   Brian Winston's candid film *A Boatload of Wild Irishmen* (2011) shows the compromises that Flaherty made. Aran islanders spoke Gaelic, but Flaherty recorded the soundtrack in London in English. Nonetheless, Flaherty's vision of Aran has triumphed – the island is a tourist spot dedicated to his film, drawing thousands each year.

it can be argued that Dziga Vertov's constructivist experiments and the kitsch expressions of Nazism to be found in Leni Riefenstahl's œuvre contributed to the evolution of documentaries in the 1920s and 1930s.[13] But one has only to venture such an assertion in order to realise how, in relation to what was going on in written journalism or photography, the evolution of documentary was faltering, painfully slow.

In some respects the problems arose from the limitations of technology. Robert Capa's war photographs were taken with a Leica, a small, elegantly designed object not so different from contemporary cameras. For the most part, movie cameras were bulkier and unwieldy, ill-suited to capturing reality. (Capa did use a small camera to record moving pictures during the Spanish Civil War, but his efforts, as indeed his efforts to make documentary films during the 1950s, are curiously disappointing.) Synchronous sound was recorded on discs with machinery that fitted neatly in a medium-sized truck. But the cramp placed on the form by ideology proved to be just as important.

This was apparent even within the relative freedoms of the 'soft' propaganda pioneered by John Grierson, first at Britain's Empire Marketing Board, then at the General Post Office (GPO). A Scottish Calvinist, Grierson remains a controversial figure. Some regard him as the progenitor of socially conscious film, others point to a bullying prescriptiveness in relation to the proper subject matter of documentaries. Grierson was, above all, a propagandist. He wanted to see films capable of changing the world. 'There was no question where one's duty lay,' he explained. 'There was no question that it started out in a political conception, a political, social conception.' Grierson paid his dues to the spirit of extreme literalism. ('There's nothing like the camera for getting around,' he explained helpfully. 'That's what makes it unique, the fact that it can travel from place to place.') Most damaging, perhaps, were the compromises with his paymasters over the question of how his subjects should be depicted. Prudently, in his position among the social democrats or One Nation Tories of the British cultural establishment, Grierson decided that films should reflect the 'interdependence' of humans. This meant that his school shied away from overt class-war propaganda. But it also perpetuated a woozy propagandist worldview in which poor people were patronised, somewhat in the style of contemporary 'one world' social commentary, with its obsessional focus on the 'flatness' of the world at the expense of human difference.[14]

---

13   Those interested in the pushiness and bad faith of Leni Riefenstahl can consult Stephen Bach's *Leni* (Little, Brown, 2005), a rigorous and convincing investigation conducted wholly without malice. A brief attempt to rehabilitate Riefenstahl was made in the 1970s, on the grounds that her aesthetic sense might be said to trump the many lies. Susan Sontag's essay in the *New York Review of Books* (Feb. 1975) makes the point that one can possess some aesthetic sense and still be a liar. Others may feel (as I do) that the showiness of Leni's work is at once reality-denying and terminally boring.
14   For a less critical account of Grierson's views, see Chris Durlacher's *The Documentary Film Mob* (BBC4, 2011).

In the 1930s companies like Shell funded documentaries, and they could prove surprisingly free-minded when it came to the question of whether they should impose their will on film-makers eager to make their own films. But it is hard to regard these early corporate efforts as a genuine advance of the documentary form – at their best they anticipate the films of our day funded by NGOs or companies. They bear the same resemblance to film-making that the most sophisticated PR handouts do to independent reportage.

Avant-garde works at this time were few, and overshadowed by the imperative of saving the world, or at least stopping it falling into chaos. Even when 1930s films were privately funded, however, they tended to adhere to an ideological line. It would seem indeed that at some moment the idea of documentary became near-irrevocably identified with the spirit of progressivism, linked more or less fatally, as Grierson laid down, to 'purposes'. This is true of the films of Joris Ivens, the Dutch film-maker who collaborated with Hemingway on *The Spanish Earth*, an account of fighting in the Spanish Civil War filmed from the Republican side. Ivens's subsequent career led him to espouse progressivism even when this meant excusing the crimes committed by Stalin or Mao. 'A militant documentary film has to reach further,' he said, after rejecting Hemingway's observation that writers should aim to tell the truth. 'After informing and moving audiences, it should agitate – mobilize them to be active in connection with the problems shown in the film.'[15]

How would documentaries be viewed? Could they be enlisted in efforts to change the world or were they doomed to remain a hobby of the enlightened few? Ambitions notwithstanding, documentaries were viewed by pitifully small audiences – and usually consisting of the already engaged. The delusion survives to this day, in the notion that films made for a small left-wing audience can somehow change the world. It has given birth to the proposition, never fully discussed, that documentary is inherently a left-wing or social democratic form, based on the idea that documentary films are collective enterprises, and somehow lend themselves to the promotion of collective effort.

The earliest effort to take documentaries out of specialist film clubs into the developing mass media came from Henry Luce's news magazine *Time*. Luce had the idea of extending his own popular print format into film, and he employed a team to create films that could be shown before the main feature but were longer than newsreels. Luce didn't make the additional fortune he had hoped for from *The March of Time*, but the films were successful as a marketing device, reaching 20 million Americans each week. *March of Time* films can nowadays be viewed online, through the archive of Time Warner. Once one gets used to the crashing music and the pompous corporate voice, many of the films feel surprisingly fresh. Writing in the *Guardian*, Alistair

---

15   Macdonald and Cousins, *Imagining Reality,* 140.

Cooke referred to the London premiere of *The March of Time* as 'far and away the most important thing that has happened for years'. Critics did complain of the sensationalism of the series, observing that content was usually subordinated to narrative requirements. But in the 1930s, significantly, it was Luce's apparent lack of ideological bias that appeared offensive to liberal commentators such as Frank Crowninshield, the founding editor of *Vanity Fair*. Less apparent at the time was the frequent use of amateur actors in reconstructions. Haile Selassie was played by a *Time* office boy. For *Inside Nazi Germany* (1938), the film-makers went to German neighbourhoods in Hoboken, using American streets to depict German cities in which Jewish stores and residences had been effaced by daubed swastikas.[16] Innovations such as these, which, for better or worse, have come to define much of contemporary broadcast journalism, were introduced without fuss or prior consultation. It would seem that nobody complained.

During the Second World War newsreels were shown weekly to vast audiences, but many of these resembled the weekly hate speech moments commemorated in *1984* – they were artefacts concocted for fixed purposes, to elicit hate or appreciation, to educate in the least-defined way, or convey propaganda. Documentaries were somewhat rarer, and they were expected to join in the task of raising morale. Films from the school of Grierson did just this, and the interdependence ethos fitted easily with the all-in-khaki one-size-fits-all wartime cultural egalitarianism voiced at the time by Orwell in *The Lion and the Unicorn,* among others. The most interesting ventures of the time, however, are those of Humphrey Jennings, a Cambridge aesthete, poet, photographer, and fan of the continental surrealists, whose work didn't always find favour with more earnest agitprop colleagues. *Fires Were Started* (1943) unaffectedly and with great observational sophistication substitutes for wartime uplift the eccentricity of the British. In a similar way to the Powell and Pressburger feature film *The Life and Death of Colonel Blimp* (1943), Jennings shows what the British may have been fighting for, half-unawares.

A Diary for Timothy (1945), Jennings's masterpiece, is one of the few films to explain, through the device of a wartime diary kept on behalf of a newborn, scripted by E. M. Forster, what postwar Britain should be like. Not through statistics or assertion, but poetically, with wide-eyed wonder, Jennings raises the possibility that through social democracy people might learn to look after each other. But there were limitations to Jennings's approach. It was Forster who complained about the patronising, class-based aspects of the draft script submitted to him. ('Tim', he fussed, 'must be someone, and why shouldn't he be born in a rectory and have a lovely choral baptism instead of being

16   James L. Baughman, *Henry Luce and the Rise of the American News Media* (Johns Hopkins University Press, 1987), 79–80.

an industrialist [sic] baby at a registry office.'[17]) In the final version, Michael Redgrave's plummy condescension appears to smother poor Timothy in his NHS cot:

Well, dear Tim, that's what's been happening around you...
and you see it's only by chance that you're safe and sound.
Up to now we've done the talking, but before long you'll sit up
and take notice. What are you going to say about it and what
are you going to do? You heard what Goronwy was thinking –
underemployment after the war and then another war... Will
it be like that again? Are you going to have greed for money
and power ousting decency from the world as they have in
the past? Or are you going to make the world a different place
– you and all the other babies?[18]

It requires an unusual, brave talent to make films capable of rendering the possibilities of life. To our day, plodding films about the circumstances of poverty, of the kind favoured by Jennings's colleagues in the Crown Film Unit,[19] are far more common.

Another wartime innovation, however, was to prove more significant, and this was the alarm of state patrons in the army or civil service when confronted by material deemed likely to upset or destabilise audiences or powerful bosses. Much of the most explicit wartime coverage from the 1940s wasn't shown until many years later.[20] This proved to be the fate of the ten-minute film that the film lover and cinema owner Sidney Bernstein caused to be shot in 1945, after the liberation of Belsen, in which one can see heaped-up, emaciated corpses and a choked-up British sergeant telling a group of rounded-up German civilians that what he has seen is a disgrace. The showing of John Huston's *The Battle of San Pietro* (1945), which gives an unvarnished, wrenching account of the carnage involved in taking a small Italian town, was delayed for a year as his army patrons pondered its negative message. His next film *Let There be Light*, for which he spent three months in the veterans' ward of the Mason General Hospital, shooting 375,000 feet of film, now seems to be a wholly uncontroversial venture but it was never shown. The US Army gave a number of reasons, none of them convincing. It would appear that they

17 Kevin Jackson, *Humphrey Jennings* (Picador, 2004), 304.
18 Ibid. 301.
19 The Crown Film Unit was created as a successor to the GPO (Post Office) Film Unit in 1940. Its function was to supply wartime propaganda for the Home Front.
20 Uncovering compromising archive became a minor industry during the 1960s. Claude Chabrol's *L'Œil de Vichy* (1993) recreates the experience of sitting through the skilled lies of pro-German propagandists. More subtly, *The Sorrow and the Pity* (1969; see below p. 45) shows in counterpoint the different tone of German, French, and British propaganda. Connoisseurs of the genre will enjoy Alfred Knobler's *Le Bonheur dans vingt ans* (1972), a compilation of Stalinist newsreels that stops just short of the arrival of the Russian tanks in 1968.

had never wished to fund anything as frank, or indeed as frankly upsetting.

A consensus developed that ended by placing restrictions on the scope of documentary films. Factual films were useful, and thus desirable, it was thought, but they should stay within certain limits. Postwar documentaries were presumed to improve audiences, and they were a social democratic alternative to the propaganda emanating from dictatorships. Planning, housing, poverty – these are the approved subjects of early documentary film, with the odd mail train belching smoke thrown in for poetry. The redoubtable Denis Forman, who began his career at the Orwellian-named COI (Central Office of Information), later becoming the inspiration of Granada television's factual programmes, captures the atmosphere:

> *Many of the film-makers… were fellow-travellers or communist sympathisers… As a result they would throw in morsels of left-wing propaganda which had nothing to do with the topic in hand. For instance a film on the history of domestic architecture paused when it reached a servants' bedroom in a great town house to deliver a homily on the wretched way in which the aristocracy had treated the lower classes.*[21]

There was no commercial market for factual film, and the financing of documentary film required public bodies. They might be government information services, public bodies set up to support documentary, public television stations, or networks given public obligations – whichever was the case, documentaries were anchored in a culture of well-meaning left-of-centre pedagogy. They were meant not exactly to change the world – that would have seemed too ambitious – but to act as a conscience. At their most ambitious they were seen as warning signs giving notice of what might go wrong. 'Problems' or 'issues' were the fittest subjects for documentaries – most safely within such contemporary preoccupations as housing, health, education, etc. Those who made documentaries wrestled with this orthodoxy, but they accepted it, too. They also acquired a significant degree of freedom. It became customary for film-makers to define their work in opposition to the ostensibly value-free news bulletins shown each night. Authorship of documentaries was thus defined in the most conservative, left-wing style – you were an author to the degree that your work succeeded in pressing the correct social buttons, thus arousing the faithful.

The history of postwar broadcasting is marked by small-scale battles in which producers are pitted against the authorities. At the time such struggles supplied much copy for those writing about television. They seemed to arise

---

21   Denis Forman, *Persona Granada* (Andre Deutsch, 1997), 19.

from and illustrate the perception that this relatively new medium offered the possibility of unique powers of persuasion. The new guardians – television executives, bureaucrats from the regulatory authorities set up to supervise the new medium, self-styled keepers of morality, and, of course, politicians – insisted that different rules should apply to those using the medium of film. Film-makers weren't like journalists – because television was more powerful, and because unlike journalists they worked in a tightly regulated industry. But film was also deemed to be unreliable. Compared to print it was a slippery medium, liable to slide towards propaganda unless properly supervised. For would-be censors the tendency of film-makers to introduce their own views into their films was something to be guarded against. Nowadays, with the unfettered internet, such conflicts seem impossibly distant. But they were important, not least because they determined how people thought about the potential of television. They also determined the erratic development of documentaries, delaying acceptance of a form in which one could say much of what one wanted.

Among the most notorious struggles was the one that took place within the recently created CBS News, at the height of the Cold War. It was centred around the figure of Edward R. Murrow. So much has been written about Murrow, so much of it excessively praising him, that it may now be necessary to remind readers that he was above all, in addition to his many other qualities of charm, courage, grace under persistence, and awesome stubbornness, an extremely good reporter. It was indeed Murrow who almost alone revealed the possibilities of modern broadcast journalism. He was born in South Carolina and brought up in Washington State, far away from the media centres of New York and Washington. Murrow was, from the beginning, more than a mere reporter. He had worked for organisations promoting asylum for refugee academics from Hitler's Germany. Briefly, he arranged tours of the curious to Stalin's Russia. Never swayed by the charms of Soviet Russia, Murrow, British suits, wing tips, and aristocratic mistress notwithstanding, was a New Dealer and an activist of sorts, who had come early to comprehend the enormous power (for bad as well as good) of the mass media.

People should study Murrow's broadcasts in order to appreciate the strong effects achieved by minimalist prose. But they also show how far one can stray from the impositions of 'objectivity' without quite seeming ever to wholly cross the line into engagement. His extraordinary scripting skills came from radio experience in the 1930s and 1940s where he witnessed the collapse of the European order, the Blitz, and the liberation of the camps. Murrow had encountered the dictators of Europe at first hand, and viewed with great contempt the efforts of politicians to dominate television. But he also believed that in a democracy good ideas must be helped along, lest the bad ones prevail. He would have understood and despised the efforts of Silvio Berlusconi and

Vladimir Putin to control the medium, believing that television belonged to citizens, and had a duty to support their interests rather than those of the powerful.

It is in this context that one must view his most celebrated programme, in which he attacked Senator ('Tail-gunner Joe') McCarthy. The programme was delivered live, on 9 March 1954, with Murrow reading from a script while his producers fed in excerpts from McCarthy's speeches. It feels both bizarrely crude and extraordinarily sophisticated – as if the kinoscope off-air recording were itself a documentary of sorts, describing in *verité* style a unique, unrecoverable moment in the history of mass media. Murrow had lingered long over the decision, and some have criticised him for excess of caution in not attacking McCarthy earlier. It has been suggested that he waited until the Senator was about to expose Murrow's youthful leftishness. But Murrow was as much motivated by the conventions that had grown up around the use of television as a journalistic medium. He knew that so straightforward, unqualified an attack was breaking the rules. It would offend the programme's sponsors, but also create an unacceptable precedent. Although Murrow is most remembered these days for his attacks on the crassness of television,[22] his real worry was that the medium wouldn't fund a way of accommodating either the reality of persistent controversy or, worse still, the plurality of voices required in any democracy. 'Politicians, whoever they are, should not be permitted to control television,' he said in a lecture sponsored by Granada Television in 1961. 'Let them use it, let them be as persuasive as they may be, but do not permit them to use this instrument to prevent today's minority from becoming tomorrow's majority.'[23]

Significantly, however, Murrow's victory turned out to be short-lived. *See it Now*, the current affairs series which he and Fred Friendly had pioneered in the teeth of network misgivings, was axed. Murrow's subsequent reports for the network are proficient and worthy, focusing on the usual themes of liberal journalism, but are a pale shadow of the McCarthy onslaught. And Murrow appears to have given up the fight for the non-existent soul of commercial television. He finally left CBS to become JFK's head of USIA, succumbing to the lure of Camelot and producing New Frontier propaganda that he neither

---

22   In *Good Night and Good Luck*, George Clooney's film about Murrow, this contemporary theme is played up, with an ending in which Murrow delivers his famous speech denouncing the pressures of advertising.
23   There are many accounts of Murrow's life. Still the best is A. M. Sperber, *Murrow; His Life and Times* (Freundlich Books, 1986). Murrow's joust with McCarthy is described in ch. 13 (pp 414–71). The Granada lecture is on pp. 571–3. The most convincing account of the great years of CBS is in David Halberstam's history of American media, *The Powers that Be* (University of Illinois, 2000). The treatment of CBS boss and founder Bill Paley in *Good Night and Good Luck* is highly misleading. Federal Communications Commission (FCC) rules mandated balance. Whether he wished or no, Paley was obliged to give McCarthy a right of reply and Murrow had anyhow acknowledged this in the opening sentences of his polemic. It was the requirement for a right to reply that ultimately hobbled television journalism. No proprietor, no matter how generous, would turn over large portions of lucrative airtime to those criticising programmes.

cared about excessively, nor did specially well. Murrow was made privy to the numerous lies told in the pursuit of the Vietnam War, though he kept secrets loyally, smarting all the while. Like many contemporaries he went on smoking, even after he had introduced the first film linking cancer to cigarettes, with the observation that a cure might be found in time to save his life. By the time of his death in 1965, of a lung cancer that he awaited, greeting its progress with stoic indifference, he appeared to have lost all hope in the notion that the prospects of democracy could somehow be advanced by the medium in which he had triumphed.

I once met Fred Friendly, Murrow's genial producer, who left CBS under pressure, helped devise public television in the US, and finally became Edward R. Murrow Professor of Journalism at Columbia University. 'We really didn't know what we were doing,' Friendly told me. 'And you mustn't think of us as pioneers. Most of the time it was just gluing pieces of film together. We rarely stopped to think what we were doing.' I also lunched at a midtown restaurant in Manhattan with Don Hewitt, one of the early generation of CBS, then in his 70s and still employed by the company. Hewitt had worked with Ed Murrow and Fred Friendly. He didn't want me to be too impressed by Murrow. 'He was important for his time,' Hewitt said, a little grudgingly. 'You couldn't do all that now.' The style of American election coverage, which hasn't significantly changed to this day, was largely Hewitt's doing. Hewitt created the fast-moving graphics and on-the-spot reporting of election specials. He had invented the format of *60 Minutes*, devising the language of feature news journalism. For all his surface animation, Hewitt's was the authentic voice of network caution. He had watched many documentaries, enjoying them, though he complained, like most television journalists, about the lack of balance of many documentaries. Murrow's efforts he dismissed as 'bleeding heart things'. 'They were often unfair,' he said of the celebrated CBS reports. 'Sometimes they damaged us.' Only when we were about to leave did he finally deliver his definition of a good documentary. 'It's nothing to do with the images,' he said. 'It comes down to the words. Imagine someone sitting in a living room.' Think of the viewer. He 'has to be able to get up from the couch, walk across to the wet bar, mix a drink, walk back to the sofa and sit down again – and he has to do all that without losing the story.' For Hewitt there was no suggestion of a woman controlling the TV set.

Although television has, by and large, and most of all in the United States, become an unregulated free for all, the questions posed by the experiences of Hewitt and Murrow remain. Can one say what one wants within the medium, without interference? If one does say what one wants, who will listen? The most vigorous battles in Britain occurred in and around the space occupied by *World in Action*, Granada's long-running experiment in documentary journalism launched in 1963 and a near-weekly fixture of the ITV network until 1998.

The roots of *World in Action* lay in the vigorous investigative leftish tabloid tradition of newspapers such as the *Daily Mirror*. To begin with, the programme appeared to cultivate an anti-style as it attempted, edition after edition, to hit out at anything its creators found to be corrupt or inept in British society. The success of *World in Action* was made possible by a leftish management, headed by the redoubtable entrepreneur and cinema operator Sidney Bernstein. After a rocky start it was cushioned by the monopoly profits of commercial television. But the programme's progress was characterised by ceaseless battles with the regulatory authorities, which the company appeared to relish even when money was wasted in the pursuit of controversy. 'Part of its success was owed to the fact that the Granada team . . . refused to succumb to the moral blackmail through which the British establishment seeks to smother any story that could cause them embarrassment,' Denis Forman recalled.

> *Time and time again we would be told that a forthcoming programme would be against the national interest, would damage irrevocably our foreign trade, or would cause a loss of confidence in the police force, the army or the navy, and we became accustomed to listening to heavy breathing from top civil servants, from Ministers, sometimes from lawyers.*[24]

To their credit, Bernstein and his colleagues stood behind their creation. But it was the status of Granada as a protected monopoly, on which public service obligations had been imposed by law, that allowed them to do so.

World in Action reached its peak in the 1960s, when its style of grainy immediacy came to define the decade, in the same way that news magazines and photojournalism had appeared to describe the 1940s. In the 1970s it excelled once again, and was able to confront the decline of Britain with a series of investigative pieces that make most contemporary television appear half-hearted and evasive. Through *World in Action* Granada developed the idea of the documentary drama, in which actors were used when it was impossible to film an event. Docudrama is widespread now, and it often seems to do no more than claim a degree of authenticity for a film that is in its essentials fictional. The first Granada documentary dramas were stark affairs, telling the story of the meetings between Czech politicians and the Soviet Politburo in 1968, or the mistreatment of Russian dissidents. 'They were made with next to nothing,' says Leslie Woodhead. 'This was an experiment we were engaged in. How did we tell what happened when no film existed? We went to an abandoned warehouse with some actors. There was a script truly based on real documents. And we did our best.'

24   Forman, *Persona Granada,* 169.

It is interesting to compare the Granada style with the BBC's efforts. The BBC laboured under the burdens of the obligation to be impartial, but even when such allowances are made, 1960s and 1970s editions of *Panorama* appear gratuitously starchy and over-keen to appear authoritative. Good reporting was to be found on the magazine show *24 Hours*, which reflected the upheavals of the 1960s. Genuine flair and freshness, however, came from the individual voices of talented reporters, among them the remarkably stubborn Charles Wheeler and James Mossman, an ex-spy and homosexual with a Le Carréish end-of-empire view of the world who combined great writing skills with a film-maker's sensibility. In Nicholas Wright's play *The Reporter* (2007) the character based on Mossman tells how it was in the glory days of the BBC:

> *In those days of innocence I used to record my voiceovers in*
> *hotel lavatories with blankets over the window to deaden*
> *the traffic noise. Then I'd pack up the film, the tapes, the*
> *cutting order and send it to London like a Christmas parcel.*
> *Days later a telex might arrive, laconic, brief: 'Your story*
> *transmitted, twelve minutes.' Very occasionally, 'Well done.'*
> *The only time I saw the film myself was when I returned to*
> *London. Then I'd watch on a monitor in Lime Grove Studios,*
> *a leaking hell-hole at the back of Shepherd's Bush Green,*
> *tenaciously clung to over the years on the grounds that*
> *outward luxury would be superfluous to a department so*
> *superior to any other as BBC current affairs.*[25]

Mossman's films now appear a curious blend of sophisticated, often wayward scripts, with remarkable images, wildly unevenly edited.[26] But his own voice is what lingers long afterwards. He was permitted to have views, and the images he sent back weren't excessively repackaged. In the long-running series *One Pair of Eyes* the BBC continued with the tradition of the reporter-observer through the 1960s and 1970s. Nowadays such overtly small-audience, elitist experiments are hard to find on television. Polemics have replaced the more leisurely observational style. But one would have to conclude that investigative journalism, despite many efforts, was never the BBC's forte. As late as 1981, documents recently released reveal the Director-General, Sir Ian Trethowan, felt obliged to send a *Panorama* dealing with the British secret services to the legal officer of MI5 for advice. He passed on the many suggested cuts to the programme's editor. During the 2008 Hutton inquiry, which dealt with the BBC's coverage of the famous Blair memo stating that Iraq was in possession

25   Nicholas Wright, *The Reporter* (Nick Hern Books, 2007), 7.
26   See for instance his essay on Cuba, *Panorama*, 29 Oct. 1962, BBC archive online.

of lethal weapons, there were many (including the judge) who appeared to think that the BBC had no business looking into such things. As a national, public broadcaster, it should restrict itself to news already public, acting as a recorder of the national debate rather than breaking stories.

The most daring piece of investigative journalism of the Thatcher era proved to be a documentary aired in the series *This Week* by Thames Television. It described the shooting of three IRA members by an SAS squad. The IRA members were unarmed, but one of them had just parked a car adjacent to the parade ground where a parade was due to take place the following Monday. The programme concluded that they hadn't provoked the SAS squad, and that their killing was preventive, part of a Shoot To Kill policy adopted against the IRA. After the Home Office tried unsuccessfully to get the regulators to censor the programme, Mrs Thatcher and her ministers went on the attack, supported by titles of the Murdoch press, including *The Sunday Times* and the *Sun*. A later inquiry organised by Thames Television supported the programme's conclusions. Soon after, however, the Thatcher government, in what seemed to many at the time to be an act of revenge against the presumption of independent television, instituted the auction of licences, making it harder for companies to spend large sums of money on journalism. Thames Television, which bid unwisely low, lost its franchise.[27]

There had been some small degree of recognition for Granada's efforts, as it became recognised that the company brought serious journalism to television. In the end, however, *World in Action* was laid low by managerial apathy. When the company was finally taken over, it was long past its prime. Audiences had become less receptive to the idea that television should fulfil the mission of Granada's founders. The fate of *World in Action* does pose the question of what, ultimately, can be achieved by critical documentary journalism. For most of its long life the programme wasn't a drain on Granada's finances. It wasn't infrequent to see the programme in ITV's top ten shows, with audiences of over ten million. *World in Action* did contribute, along with *The Sunday Times*, at that moment one of the world's great newspapers, to the decline in deference in mid-century Britain. Ultimately, however, the tradition of filmed investigations faltered and died in Britain, as indeed it has elsewhere.

Contemporary political television does offer the illusion of great freedom. It would seem indeed, if you look at the polemic-stuffed shows of cable television in the US, that no one need complain about excessive political control of television. But the voices come from wholly predictable corners, often stifling public debate even as they appear to be encouraging it. It is difficult to argue that the new market-led television has delivered any degree of pluralism or even significantly enhanced the marketplace of political ideas.

27   David Elstein, *Open Democracy*, 23 Nov. 2009.

Among the middle-aged, disgruntled television executives who crowd conferences, therefore, the 1970s remain a Golden Decade of television. There weren't many channels and the perceived restriction of consumer choice was utilised to force commercial quasi-monopolies to sustain a tradition of public service. Within the BBC the tradition of public education survived, too. Although there were frequent collisions between those brought up in the 1960s and their elders, who now administered the system, a great expansion of original programming occurred.[28] The principal beneficiaries of this situation were factual programme-makers, who could choose a variety of departments in which to work. Within these pieces of a sprawling bureaucracy one might spend a portion of a lifetime working on such series as *Timewatch* (history with a popular slant), *Horizon* (hard science), *Man Alive* (tabloid human interest), *Forty Minutes* (less tabloid human interest), *Omnibus* and *Arena* (mainstream arts, and quirkier essay films*)*, *The South Bank Show* (more art but on ITV, by no means always lacking in challenge), or *Panorama* (current affairs, still made for the elite, mostly by members of the elite). The most remarkable instance of subsidised highbrow television was Granada's *Disappearing World*, a series of anthropological films that ran for 15 years, few of which could now be funded or even shown outside a digital channel. Each season of television fare contained at least one longish series on a subject of importance. Sometimes, like *The World at War* (Thames, 1973–4) which described the Second World War, running to 26 episodes, and *The People's Century* (BBC/WGBH, 1990), these took many years to make, costing millions of pounds. The creation of Channel Four in 1981 came in part as a response to the pressures of independent film-makers who wanted to secure access to channels. They suggested that their programmes would bring new voices to television. This proved to be the case. To begin with, the new channel introduced a degree of freshness and risk into what had become a staid duopolistic system. It attracted people who couldn't stand to work at the BBC and ITV. With respect to documentaries, the new channel specialised in opinionated reporting. But it also began to show international work, without editing it.[29] For the first time British audiences became aware of the variety of styles with which documentaries were made all over the world. The channel came to evolve in a direction of greater reliability. What had once seemed innovation became, in due course and without excessive fanfare or surprise,

28 The most elaborate system of public/private collaboration was in Britain, where ITV came to imitate both the organisation and the editorial style of the BBC. Similar systems had grown up in Canada, Germany, Japan. Even in France, where censorship was still routinely exercised, a strongly educative public interest ethos prevailed. In America, too, the networks retained large staffs committed to public interest television.
29 A personal note: it was thanks to Channel Four, at which the documentary series *True Stories* had been created, that I was encouraged to create Storyville, showing international documentaries on the BBC. Working for Channel Four during the 1980s I was able to make and then commission hundreds of hours of documentaries, in circumstances of total freedom. In its earliest incarnation the channel gave unmatched opportunities to those eager to take risks in the quest of making provocative programmes.

a marketing style. By the first years of the new century, the channel was notorious not for its abrasive comedies, or unusual documentaries, but for the ratings- and money-gathering *Big Brother* – the most successful of the many 'reality shows' into which its original quest to describe the world differently had morphed. The long-term effect of Channel Four was, more simply, choice. In the end what Channel Four came to offer was more television, good or bad. It didn't change the culture of television as much as its admirers had hoped.

No one should belittle the great, long moment of public television. Something of its flavour is preserved in Robert Hughes's autobiographical essay:

> *The mid-sixties was, in my recollection, a wonderful time for intelligent and serious TV in England. In Beeb-Two I never heard the word 'ratings' mentioned. It was simply assumed that you did your best to create high-quality programming for reasonably intelligent viewers, to whom you did not condescend. The saber-toothed technocrats who would presently move in on the medium were not yet born, or at least not raised. The talent in and around the organization was not yet ashamed of its aspirations or, as the Murdoch boys and girls would call them now, its 'pretensions.'*[30]

These were indeed spectacular years, and amid the dross of the schedule viewers could encounter many remarkable programmes of enduring value, within what the dramatist Dennis Potter called the 'palace of varieties in the corner of the room,'[31] night by night. It may seem invidious to wish to single out any one film from the multitude of public service broadcasting offerings, but I recall *The Two Winstons*, the last episode of Simon Schama's *A History of Britain* (2000). This wasn't a lecture, but, in the approved style of BBC programmes, featuring an onscreen literate presenter and many carefully filmed locations, scripted down to the last pause, it also wasn't quite a film. Daringly, however, it rendered the two lives of George Orwell and Winston Churchill side by side in an hour through the device of Orwell's use of the latter's name in *1984*. An attentive viewer could find out a lot about the more appealing side of Churchill (Schama recalled his funeral in particular, which he experienced as a teenager, not at that moment a great admirer of the Old Imperialist) and something of the dogged ultimate persistence in truth of Orwell, creator, like Churchill, of great national myths. If you want to know anything about the country you inhabit, the programme suggested, it's all

30   Robert Hughes, *Things I Didn't Know* (Harvill Secker, 2006), 323.
31   McTaggart lecture, Edinburgh Television Festival (1993), among the most embittered, impassioned defences of public television against the encroachment of the market. Potter knew he was dying when he gave the lecture, and he was visibly in pain.

here. And so indeed it was.

Think of the documentary output of the BBC in any one year, from the mid-1960s through to the 1990s. Aside from the 'strands' listed above there were series. These were crafted for the two channels, BBC1 and BBC2. Each series was carefully researched, filmed with care. In department meetings (those I attended were at the end of this era, when the BBC was under pressure to commission more from independents) no one discussed how a film might be made or what it should say. Instead we talked about the limited number of institutions still to be penetrated by the BBC. The house ethos and indeed style was ultra-Griersonian. We should indeed seek to express the 'interdependence' of those who lived in Britain. It was acceptable to criticise incompetence in government, or to draw attention to unfulfilled expectations, but our tone must remain impartial. Much attention, understandably, was paid to the avoidance of fakery. One shouldn't criticise the rote aspect of much of this output. As the producer and executive Peter Dale has observed, throughout the 1970s and 1980s and even into the 1990s 'millions of British television viewers sat down to well-crafted, insightful and often moving documentaries about themselves and their neighbours . . . they were appointments to view for a postwar society keen to explore new ideas, faces, ways of living – a sense of what it is to live in a liberal and tolerant society'.[32] Taken as a whole, television documentary in Britain proved to be a comprehensive portrait of its time. We'll never know how it altered the perspective of viewers, but it seems safe to assume that many of those who watched the output came to agree with at least some of the predominantly liberal viewers of the producers and directors who made the films.

Anyone seeking to understand the great change that came over British broadcasting with the decline of the public service ethos should consider the fate of the successive documentaries made about the Queen and the royal family. The first of these, *Royal Family*, 105 minutes long, was screened in 1969, and it was made by the then head of documentaries at the BBC, Richard Cawston. To the astonishment of Her Majesty's subjects and the 100-odd million audience who watched the film throughout the world, the Royals were shown watching television, having breakfast, and awkwardly preparing a barbecue. When they weren't bemused by the banality of royal lives, viewers appeared content with what they saw. But there were those who thought that the film was a mistake – because, in the idiom of contemporary documentaries, it showed that the Royals were rather like us. 'Initially the public will love seeing the Royal Family as not essentially different from anyone else and in the short term letting in the cameras will enhance the Monarchy's popularity,' remarked the commentator Peregrine Worsthorne

---

32   Peter Dale, personal communication.

presciently. 'But in the not-so-long run familiarity will breed, if not contempt, familiarity.'[33] Although *Elizabeth R*, a 1992 royal portrait, passed off without incident, Worsthorne's observations were on the mark, and the royal family rapidly became implicated, willy-nilly, in the celebritisation of British mass culture. Princess Diana used the famous *Panorama* interview not just to make public her marital problems but to criticise the hauteur of the Windsors. *A Year with the Queen* (2007) paid due homage to these developments. This wasn't an exercise in 'fly-on-the-wall' film-making. Instead, it resembled in its utter absence of intimacy the formalised picture spreads to be found each week in *Hello* magazine. Its lack of ambition notwithstanding, the series proved troublesome for the BBC – because its producers, in making a promo tape for purchasers, made it appear that the Queen had walked out in a huff of a photo session with the photographer Annie Leibowitz.[34]

To many print journalists, whose own methodology left much to be desired, the failings of documentaries were a sign of the frivolity of television and the inadequacy of documentary as a journalistic form. In reality, however, the offences committed by film-makers were relatively modest, and most documentaries stayed honest. But one can look at the triumph of popular television, and what observers perceived to be the relentless decline in standards, from a slightly different angle.[35] From the vantage point of the history of documentaries, so marred by insecurity, television seemed more than a haven. But there were also those who insisted, year after year, that television was bad for their work, and that there was a huge price to be paid when one worked for the medium. Wasn't so much material in reality a substitute for the freer, more radical things that might have happened with less control? Would it be possible to envisage a genuinely free television? These were the so-called independent film-makers. Although they worked at the margins of what still appeared to be the most marginal of forms, their views became steadily more and more important.

33 In case anyone had missed it, *Royal Family* was shown the following week on ITV. It has not since been screened in full.
34 A report commissioned by the BBC blamed the production company RDF, adding, perhaps redundantly, that it was unlikely that 'anyone consciously set out to defame or misrepresent the Queen in the tape'. Both Peter Fincham, the Controller of BBC1, who had introduced the tape at a launch with reference to the Queen's ill temper, and the chief creative officer of RDF, Stephen Lambert, resigned. The series was retitled *Monarchy: The Royal Family at Work* and shown to general approval.
35 The fullest account of the fall of ITV is Ray Fitzwalter's *The Dream that Died* (Matador, 2008). Fitzwalter was one of the best editors of *World In Action*, and he sees the events that followed the 1990 decision to auction ITV franchises as a publicly sanctioned act of vandalism. Could ITV under other circumstances have sustained a degree of public mission? Fitzwalter thinks it could have done. More convincingly than others, he argues that the BBC and Channel Four are not alone capable of fulfilling the sort of educational obligations required in a medium as important as television.

3. Indie Documentaries: film as a life's work

Like most cultural terms that enter public discourse, the notion of 'independent' film implies a degree of wish fulfilment. Films are expensive to make and even now require some sort of industrial support – distributors, publicists, cinema projectors, popcorn vendors, etc. Most so-called 'indie' films are these days in part funded by the studios from whose clutches they were supposed to have escaped. But in the 1960s it was still possible to believe that films might be made 'outside the system'. They would be created with small budgets, financed by different sources – distributors might be prepared to invest, but there were also wealthy individuals – and shown in small cinemas. They would be different from Hollywood fare – less bland, more attuned to the tastes of young people. And they would also foster the amalgam of lifestyle and politics in evidence on the streets.

Additionally, two sets of technical developments separated by 20 years made it possible to think of independently produced, coherently authored documentaries. The first occurred in the early 1960s, when lighter 16 millimetre cameras were available, with synchronised sound, courtesy of a lightweight recorder known as a Nagra.[36] New and faster stock made it possible to do without lights, though it was still necessary to reload the camera every ten minutes. But a film-maker could hang around his or her subjects for longer. Reality could now be stalked and captured. The second came when a variety of cameras using tape came on the market, starting in the 1980s. Filming costs fell dramatically, and cameras became smaller and smaller, easier to use. Now it was possible to film for up to an hour. Lights weren't required, and the camera was small enough not to be noticed. (These days it is possible to do without tape, using a hard drive in the camera, transferring images to a laptop.) It was cumbersome to edit

---

36 The inventions required are described in *The Camera that Changed the World*, Lambent Productions, directed by Mandy Chang (BBC4, 2011).

tape, but by the early 1990s random access editing was freely available.[37] This meant that you didn't have to spin backwards and forwards while assembling a film. You could store drafts, discarded sequences. And it was possible by using a keyboard to construct faster-moving sequences more rapidly.

Most of these innovations are cheap, very easy to use, and they have fully democratised the process of telling stories on film.[38] They have led to an astonishing explosion in documentary film-making as, decade by decade, film-makers have seized the new technology, fashioning it to their own purposes. It now requires some imagination to recall what things were like before these inventions. But one must remember, too, the part played by the development in parallel of more sophisticated means of showing films. In the 1960s, films were shown on celluloid. Often, faced with a deadline, the cutting copy, scarred and scratched with the joints over which a substance barely more durable than sellotape was clearly visible, was used for television showings. It was rare to watch documentaries that had been transferred to tape, and the picture quality of tape was too poor for showing in cinemas. In the 1980s VHS technology made it possible for the first time to hand films around so that they could be shown at leisure, outside television schedules. But the picture quality was very poor, barely good enough for university seminars. DVDs came only in the 1990s, and digital projection in cinemas still later. It is now easy to transfer films via the internet (and to download them illegally, of course).

It would be wrong to attribute so many innovations in documentary film to these developments. Something else was required, and this was the idea that a film, though collaborative, requiring many hands, was nonetheless an authored artefact. And this was as much an effect of the zeitgeist as it was a consequence of the technology. In the 1960s it became first fashionable and then normal to think about the role or function of whoever was telling a story. The New Journalism, pioneered in the United States by the likes of Tom Wolfe, Norman Mailer, and Joan Didion, sanctioned the presence of reporters in stories. It also encouraged the use of devices previously restricted to fiction – flashbacks, psychological nuance expressed through the recreation of characters' feelings, and, most important, the creation of character as well as action – thus transforming non-fiction narrative. Similar attitudes made their way into documentary film. Now the film-maker was allowed to be an author. In compensation, however, and slightly confusingly, he or she was tied

37   The most popular technology is AVID, pioneered in 1987 and brought into general use by 1992. AVID is used for feature films, but documentary film-makers were among the first to see its possibilities.

38   A good 16 millimetre camera cost upwards of £30,000 in today's prices. Although the most expensive new digital cameras cost around £8,000, cheaper models provide images good enough for theatrical viewing. Film required processing, and in the BBC it was carefully rationed. A ratio of ten minutes shot to one minute used was considered extravagant. The low cost of tape means that one can now shoot as much as one wants. It is not unusual to find that a 90 minute film has been edited out of 200 hours of material.

more tightly to the literal depiction of reality. The relationship between reality and documentary film, far from being problematic, as it had been in the past, became crucial. Films were admired to the degree that they could be said to be truthful. In the US proponents of the new documentary film-making referred to their work as Direct Cinema. In France it was known as *Cinéma Verité*. In Britain its equivalent had been known as Free Cinema.[39]

Nowadays, these innovations are lumped together so it may be as well to pause, in order to distinguish the Anglo-American 1960s school from the French one. In France *Cinéma Verité* exalted a combination of the camera's eye, and the intellect of the film-maker. It was thought that the camera was more capable of depicting truth than the erratic, instantly misremembered movements of the human eye. At the same time critics agreed that film-makers should feel free to intervene in the process of filming and editing. How they did so – how indeed one became an 'auteur' – should always be made explicit. The early practitioners of Direct Cinema were more literally minded. They introduced authenticity into film-making by drawing up 'a kind of filmic ten commandments'.[40] One must not rehearse or interview subjects. There must be no lighting, no commentary, no making subjects walk up and down or redo scenes, no lighting or staging of events, no use of dissolves while editing. Among purists at least, it was agreed that there should be no use of music to enhance emotional impact or disguise dull moments. Neither set of prescriptions endured, but they have led to two different traditions which continue to this day.

Many early adherents of *Cinéma Verité* – Jean Rouch, Chris Marker, even Alain Resnais – are forgotten outside the film academy, and this is a pity, because many of their innovations still feel fresh. For some idea of their influence, one must go to Jean-Luc Godard's essayistic collages of fact and fiction. 'Cinema is truth twenty-four times a second,' Godard famously declared. A film collective founded by him was named after Dziga Vertov in homage to the great Russian's disregard of conventional film grammar and willingness to be didactic. In *One Plus One*, filmed in London in 1968, Godard cuts from the Rolling Stones recording of 'Sympathy for the Devil' to some Black Power revolutionaries, and to a reading of *Mein Kampf* in a pornographic bookstore, interspersing footage of his own girlfriend of the day who plays a character called Eve Democracy. He appears in the last scene of the film, bespectacled and earnest, waving black and red flags.[41]

---

39 The Free Cinema movement was founded in the mid-1950s by Lindsay Anderson, with Tony Richardson and Karel Reisz. In their modest, black-and-white films, eschewing bourgeois subjects in favour of an unadorned depiction of working-class life, they prefigure not only 1960s documentaries but the great fiction films of that decade, such as Anderson's own masterpiece *This Sporting Life*.
40 Macdonald and Cousins, *Imagining Reality*, 250.
41 Colin MacCabe, *Godard* (Bloomsbury, 2003), 211–12. The film was retitled *Sympathy for the Devil* for Anglo-American audiences but it was a box office flop.

I was recently present at a sparsely attended showing of *Film Socialisme* (2011), the latest offering of the 80-year-old Godard. Superficially, nothing had changed – granddaughters of Godard's 1960s film muses perused books while slogans half-subliminally flashed on the screen. There was a long and dismally hard to read sequence shot in luridly heightened colour amid Belgian petrol pumps. Instead of the Rolling Stones, a cruise liner on which Berlusconi might have worked as a crooner served as backdrop. As it stopped at various ports, Godard used the overweight white European passengers to deliver his habitual message of the Decay of the West. The faithful stirred in their seats. Suddenly, however, with the end of the film in sight, something did appear to happen. The film didn't exactly come round to saying anything about socialism, or indeed anything else. Instead, all the elements that Godard had seemed to toy with, rearranging to his dissatisfaction, fused miraculously. All his career Godard has wanted to show that film might be used like a pen, to write in its own language. He had told us many times that film needn't consist of plodding narratives. Failing, he nonetheless bequeathed to following generations the idea that it could all be done. And here, like the faint heat from an extinct sun, was a reiteration of this promise. But the promise was illusory, and hadn't been kept. All that Godard managed to do at the end of *Film Socialisme*, as in so many of his other films, was recapitulate his own consciously stalled efforts. He had ended by constructing a narrative out of his own futile efforts to escape narrative.

Could film-makers become authors? How did they set about this task? In 1968, Louis Malle escaped from the fevered atmosphere of insurrectionary Paris, travelling to India. Until then, his own films had been somewhat staid, overcalculating depictions of bourgeois life; but in India he began to film for the first time whatever he saw. In a village where they filmed low-caste women at a well, Malle's cameraman became worried by the way in which the women looked at the camera. Malle said it didn't matter, and they should look as much they liked:

> *It's what I dislike about so many documentaries, this naïve mise en scene, the beginning of the distortion of the truth. Very quickly I realized that these looks at the camera were both disturbing and true, and we should never pretend that we weren't intruders. So we kept working that way.*[42]

Malle's series *Phantom India* (1969) is full of such scenes, and they still seem surprising. In his commentary, Malle acknowledges that he often didn't quite know what he was filming. He had been wrong about the significance of a religious ceremony or the presence of carrion crows or vultures, and he

---

42   *Malle on Malle,* ed. Philip French (Faber & Faber, 1993), 73.

had been looking for something else. The films are stronger, certainly more interesting today, for these admissions.

In 1971 I was sent to see a four-hour film then playing in a small Left Bank cinema in Paris, directed by Marcel Ophüls, a director I hadn't heard of. Finished in 1969, in the wake of the Paris upheavals, *The Sorrow and the Pity* (*Le Chagrin et la Pitié*) wasn't to be shown on French television until 1981, so afraid were the broadcasting authorities of its subversive message. It recounted the story of the Occupation of France through the eyes of the inhabitants of Clermont Ferrand, a nondescript agricultural centre slap in the middle of France, not far from Vichy. The earliest sequences set the scene in a leisurely style, with the marriage of a daughter of a German officer. Slowly the film built up the picture of a country at odds with itself by 1940, in which catastrophe was widely expected.

After the account of the 1940 collapse, told with great economy, I began to notice the crowd around me shuffling in their seats. The interview style of Marcel Ophüls was, like the film, circumlocutory and indirect, apparently meandering. He got those involved with the Nazi apparatus to talk eloquently of how they were only doing their duty. Numerous apologists recounted how Marshal Pétain had managed to spare French people by his ability to get on with the Germans. As one grim event followed another, however, and Jewish children were shipped from Paris to be murdered, these lies were apparent for what they were. Nor was the portrait of the day-to-day lives of French people any more reassuring. It was apparent that they had merely got by, most of them at least. The idea that there had been any mass support for resisting the Germans was exposed as a lie. Most of the *résistants* interviewed were outsiders – people reckless enough to have little to lose, members of the Communist party or Jews. The tone of these recollections was rueful, apologetic, non- or anti-heroic. One of the few to emerge with any credit was Pierre Mendès-France, a reforming Prime Minister in the 1950s, a Jew, and an intellectual; and he recounted how he had left occupied France to join the Free French movement, beginning with an account of how his escape from detention had nearly been frustrated by the lengthy ardours of a young couple standing against the prison wall below him as he waited to jump. All over the cinema I could hear people hissing at the screen, with freely expressed distaste if they remembered such times, in shock if they were too young.

Marcel Ophüls made many more films, including the Oscar-winning *Hotel Terminus* (1988), in which he laid bare the appalling story of the torturer Klaus Barbie, who lived hidden in exile in South America. None of his films, however, had quite the impact of *The Sorrow and the Pity*, which changed the way French people thought about their recent past, opening up discussion so that the truth about those ugly years could never again be suppressed. It was as a result of this chance viewing, with my French mother who had herself experienced the Occupation, that I first became aware of what documentaries, if they were allowed freedoms, could really do. As I've viewed the film again and again, I've asked myself how such films can still be made these days. Circumstances of course have changed since the late 1960s, and there is less intervention by politicians in the way television programmes are made and shown. But there are pressures of a different kind now, mainly economic. Also, those who administer television have become more professional. They know how audiences can only briefly be tethered to channels if one resorts to the cleverest strategies. Throughout his career Ophüls conducted a form of guerrilla war against television and its emissaries. Compare *The Sorrow and the Pity* to its near-contemporary *The World at War,* and one can conclude that, though they are both documentaries, they don't even bear a remote family resemblance. Even in its most affecting moments, *The World at War* always feels like television. It is measured, sonorous, eloquent, but muted, too. Although it attempts to account for so much atrocity, it can never quite get round to doing more than this, leaving most doors closed. Whereas, in its rambling way, through the accumulation of small, often insignificant scenes, Ophüls's film lets us in, opening door after door into the troubled past.

There have been many television accounts of the Holocaust. Television indeed became the way in which generations of Europeans, from the late 1960s, learnt about the destruction of European Jews. No narrative, however, is as strikingly, overpoweringly affecting as Claude Lanzmann's nine-and-a-half-hour-long *Shoah.* There are no archival images in *Shoah,* no reassuring commentary, and nothing seems to happen in the right order. You can frequently be irritated as you watch it. Shouldn't Lanzmann, for instance, bother to tell us that not all Poles were anti-Semites? Wouldn't it be better if he gave at least a few facts and figures? But these prove to be irrelevant considerations. Lanzmann doesn't want us to approach the murder of millions in this way. He wants us to see if it's possible to remember anything at all. If we can look at the places where the murders took place, if we can hear what those who ordered them, assisted the perpetrators, or somehow escaped death now have to say, we may understand a small portion of what happened. And if we don't, after so many hours, that won't be his fault, or indeed ours. But of course, we can and we do, and it is the great economy of means of *Shoah,* as well as its length, that makes the film so impressive. Nothing of course can be re-experienced in real time, which is how, as Proust realised, everything is indeed lost, irreparably, no matter how hard we try. But there are slivers – memories, things, shadows – that can come back, and in *Shoah* they do. When Lanzmann attempted to raise money from the American Jewish community, he was asked what the message of the film was. He replied that it had no message.

But this is the most minimal account of a film that, as Lanzmann has said in his exhaustive, fascinating account of its creation, became his life's work. Previously, he had moonlighted for the French popular press as a crime reporter while enjoying a certain Parisian notoriety as Simone de Beauvoir's live-in lover.[43] In one respect *Shoah* is the ultimate crime story, filled with perpetrators and hangers-on as well as victims. The real shock of the film, however, comes from the level of Lanzmann's own absorption in the subject matter. He recounts how long it took him to track down survivors of the Jewish Sonderkommando. He tells of the technical ingenuity required to record clandestinely the ageing Nazis unwilling to appear before a camera, and how he and his assistants risked being beaten up when they filmed through a hole in the side of a bag connected by a radio signal with a VW van parked outside. Lanzmann's book isn't an easy read, and his overly defensive, prickly tone can grate. But it is hard not to agree with him when he says that he was right not to use the inadequate archive sources for the film. 'I was faced with greatest challenge,' he says. 'I had to find a replacement for the non-existent images of death in gas chambers.'[44] When *Shoah* was first released, Lanzmann says, a 'Polish lobby' was active, criticising the hostile depiction of Poles. A minor flaw of the film may be discerned in the way in which Lanzmann appears to lead on Polish peasants, getting them to reveal their views about Jews. This is something he doesn't bother do with the many Nazi witnesses mired in evil. But these Polish peasants, though they weren't murderers, were indeed anti-Semites. With distance one can see that Lanzmann was entirely right to record the survival of a long and shameful tradition in European history.

He was surely right, too, to dismiss those critics who claimed that, by forcing witnesses to re-experience their most painful moments, he was indulging in a form of exploitation. Among the most painful moments of the film is the recollection of Abraham Bomba, whose job it was to cut the hair of the women about to be gassed. Bomba, who made his living as a hairdresser in the Bronx, is filmed cutting the hair of a friend. He recalls how he was once required to cut the hair of women from his town whom he knew. Lanzmann, anticipating that he would break down, had changed a reel of film. One can hear Bomba pleading to stop, and Lanzmann telling him he must go on:

> *The camera kept turning, Abraham's tears were as precious to me as blood, they were the hallmark of truth, its incarnation. Some have discerned in this high-risk scene a degree of some kind of sadism in myself, whereas I regard it as an ultimate expression of piety, which implies not tiptoeing backwards when you are confronted with something painful, but instead obeying the categorical imperative of finding out the truth and conveying it to others.*[45]

---

43   Claude Lanzmann, *Le Lièvre de Patagonie* (Gallimard, 2009). Translated as *The Hare of Patagonia* (Atlantic Books, 2012). References in footnotes are to the French version (author's translation).
44   Lanzmann, *Le Lièvre de Patagonie,* 437.
45   Ibid. 453.

Documentaries are often trapped within the obligation to convey detail. This can make them at best seem workmanlike. Lanzmann's film shows that if you look at something long enough and hard enough the act of description comes to be its own wholly indispensable subject. No film that I know comes as close to describing the indescribable as *Shoah*, and none, too, is as free when it comes to revealing the pain that human beings are capable of enduring, and even surviving.

I once called on Lanzmann, in his poky Left Bank apartment that doubled as an office. Maybe I should have immediately told him what I thought about his masterpiece; but I was put off by the way in which, when talking about the film, he appeared to mix up the real-life event with his own rendering of it. 'My *Shoah*' I caught him saying more than once.[46] I remember he was angry about television ('Such a stupidity! Such a waste of time!') and not well disposed towards the BBC, perhaps because the price paid for *Shoah* hadn't been specially generous. I was making a film about the far right, racists like Jean-Marie Le Pen, with whom I was spending a lot of time, and I had come to ask him what he thought about the question of how one should approach them. Did one just burst in and interview them, as I was doing? Maybe there was another, subtler way – though I couldn't see what it might be. When he learnt that I was interviewing those whom he called 'the enemy', however, he threw me out of the office. It seemed that I, too, was the enemy, coming from television. It was clear that I was betraying my trust, trivialising the most important of subjects in the quest for ratings.

Within the American documentary tradition, there are still those, most notably Fred Wiseman, who adhere to the prescriptions of the early 1960s. Others have bent the rules a bit while remaining averse to any sort of fakery. 'I have a kind of religious devotion to reality', the 85-year-old Al Maysles, who, working with his brother David, made such films as *Meet Marlon Brando* (1965), *Salesman* (1968), *Gimme Shelter* (1970), and *Gray Gardens* (1976), recently explained:

> *In religious terms, there's a wonderful word. It's called providence. Reality is providence. It provides the subjects, the subject matter and the events in their most pure and honest form. And it will continue to do so as long as we adhere to reality and let it be our boss.*[47]

---

46 Lanzmann tells us that his film ensured that henceforth the murder of European Jews would be referred to as 'the Shoah', rather than the Holocaust, which he dismisses for its implication that so many deaths possessed any degree of theological inevitability or legitimacy. He seems to claim some credit for having introduced the word. Shoah means destruction or catastrophe in Hebrew, and it would seem that it was used in this sense prior to the film. *Le Lièvre de Patagonie*, 526, and http://www.massviolence.org/Shoah, ISSN 1961-9898.

47 Interview with Peter Winttonick, Sheffield Documentary Festival Programme, June 2011.

Some scenes filmed by Maysles and his fellow practitioners are clearly set up. At the beginning of *Don't Look Back*, Don Pennebaker's 1967 portrait of Bob Dylan touring a rainy, black-and-white Britain filled with cheering girls, shady and inept promoters, and ineptly opportunistic hacks, Dylan stands in a back alley beside the Savoy Hotel, holding up cue cards with the lyrics of 'Subterranean Homesick Blues'. This is the first pop video. 'Of course we got him to do that,' Pennebaker explains. 'And we enlisted the help of the poet Allen Ginsberg. In fact the cards were his idea. We didn't know how to start the film.'[48] Elsewhere in the film, however, is a long sequence shot through the doorway of a hotel suite in which Joan Baez (Dylan's lover at the time) sings while Dylan, half-oblivious, taps out some lyrics on a portable typewriter. 'That was just being lucky,' Pennebaker recalled. He might have added that Dylan's own insouciance (he didn't insist on a contract, wouldn't be paid, and viewed the film in silence, simply saying that it was fine) was also a piece of luck, and one that wouldn't be repeated nowadays.

In view of the numerous, somewhat repetitious accusations placed at the door of documentaries, it may be worth stressing that, in these 1960s films at least, nothing is faked. In 1970, *Gimme Shelter*, the Maysles Brothers' account of the ill-fated Rolling Stones concert in Altamont, California, in which a 16 year old was bludgeoned to death by one of the Hell's Angels who had misguidedly been appointed security guards, shocked audiences. It seemed to describe how the 1960s had ended, in sordid violence; but some thought that the film also anticipated a future in which violence would be more widespread, drug-fuelled, randomly inspired, and affectless. The *New Yorker* critic Pauline Kael wrote a long attack, alleging that the film-makers, among other offences, had by their own presence caused the violence. 'There is no reason to believe that the freaked-out people in *Gimme Shelter* paid much attention to the camera crews, but would the event have taken place without those crews?' she asked.[49] Kael's charges seem contrived and excessive. Far from prophesying the Apocalypse, or writing an epitaph for the 1960s, the film describes, in astonishing detail, what happened at Altamont. As the film-makers pointed out in a letter rebutting Kael's charges, it depicts Mick Jagger's 'double self' – the strutting, campy insolence and the furies aroused in audiences by his performance. For that reason, it remains one of the great accounts of the raw power of rock and roll, even as it reminds how poorly organised concerts can end in chaos.

In the 1970s it became possible to think of documentaries as intimate

---

48 Author's interview, Sheffield Documentary Festival 2007.
49 Macdonald and Cousins, *Imagining Reality,* 274. Ibid. 455–7 for the Maysles' reply, never printed in *The New Yorker,* which in those days didn't carry readers' letters. *Gimme Shelter* was a commercial success. At the Rolling Stones' request it was withheld from British television. It was shown for the first time on BBC Storyville in 2006.

encounters with characters. *Gray Gardens* remains one of the greatest documentaries. It might appear, from the opening minutes, that the Maysles Brothers colluded with Big Edie and Little Edie, by staging the theatrical events that take place among the cats, broken furniture, and opened, rotting cans littering the near-derelict East Hampton mansion of Jackie Onassis's eccentric, impoverished relatives. But this isn't really the case at all. Little Edie requires no encouragement – from film-makers or anyone else. The film becomes hers, and she comes to own not just the audience, but the half-visible film-makers, too, who crouch in corners as she struts her stuff. As viewers (and voyeurs too) we can make up our own minds about Edie. She may be borderline mad, or very mad, or, though this sometimes seems to be a remote possibility, just pretending, fending off a life she never much liked with her act; but that doesn't mean that we can't love her as, it becomes abundantly clear, the film-makers do.

Nowadays the more original aspects of *Cinéma Verité* have shrunk even in France to a somewhat defensive, academic clinging to auteurism. The designation '*un film de*' placed at the beginning of a film is often tantamount to a health warning – something with a misplaced sense of its importance is coming your way, it seems to say. By contrast 'ob docs' or 'fly-on-the-wall' television films are everywhere. Successors of Big Edie and Little Edie are to be found not just in made-for-television contests like *X Factor* and *Big Brother*, but many only partially unfaked series (most recently, *The Only Way is Essex* is one of the most distinctive and entertaining) in which 'real life' is carefully accumulated around a predetermined plotline. But the two greatest documentary discoveries of the 1960s – that you could and should depict anything, and that someone, most likely an individual, is doing the depicting – are still relevant. Many great documentaries have been made as a consequence of these simple insights.

4.   Place in the Sun

So many great documentaries have been made and shown in recent years that it is possible to talk not of a golden age – because that would imply something static, already over – but of an explosion of new possibilities, month by month, year after year. How and why were these films made? Is there a set of explanations for the ascent of the documentary?

Cinema docs

Would documentaries ever make any money when they were released theatrically? Was there such a thing as a 'theatrical documentary'? Visiting the poky offices of New York 'documentarians', stuffed with old awards and piles of metal film cans, one might be forgiven for casting doubt on such fantasies. It is routine to find writers in the *New York Times* or elsewhere bemoaning the poor performance of documentaries, and casting doubt on their prospects of survival in the dog-eat-dog market. (The articles indeed appear as regularly as those published each year in January, each side of the Sundance Festival, acclaiming the new crop of documentary films.) In reality, there is a small market for documentaries in the US. They perform no worse than independent films, some of them grossing $5 million or over each year, and a few do very well indeed. In the former category are the films that win the Oscar, or are nominated each year. One can cite in the latter category *An Inconvenient Truth*, Al Gore's lecture about the evils of global warming, which took $24 million, and Michael Moore's *Fahrenheit 9/11* ($119 million), *Sicko* ($24 million) and *Bowling for Columbine* ($21 million).[50] But it is necessary to set these figures alongside DVD sales (though these are now falling precipitously), and, of course, income from television.

These aren't the best films of any year, to be sure. They are successful because they have been well marketed, or because their subject matter chimes with the tastes of the multiplex public. One could choose to set against the performance

50   See Appendix 2 for figures.

of a very few films the non-performance of so many others. Notwithstanding fantasies about the 'long tail' of contemporary culture, this is the fate of most documentaries, as indeed it is of most books written. Just as important as relative success or failure, however, is the fact that documentaries do receive theatrical distribution in the US.[51] This means that, within the film world, they are taken seriously, albeit as a niche form. The Oscar award is hotly contested, for instance, and documentary film-makers are noticed. Just as important, their films are able to enter the culture bloodstream in a way that they would not if they were merely shown on television, or on university campuses. And this means that the ambitions of documentaries are significantly raised. At the very least they are something more than an offshoot of the vast television industry. They can seem special now, or at least worth looking out for. You can wonder why a documentary might be on display in a multiplex, or indeed how it might be more interesting than the fictional offerings surrounding it.

In a less tangible fashion, too, documentaries have entered the surrounding film culture, making their way into what we see each year. They have become part of how we see the world. In this respect their relatively poor performance in the cinema box office is less important. It is possible to see documentaries as nudging along the rest of the culture, influencing other film-makers, writers, and activists. Documentaries are effective now not just in isolation, as a consequence of one television showing, but linked to campaigns, through the books, blogs, online articles written about them or the subjects they depict.

Hyper-real

In the 1970s, the analytical properties of television were widely touted. The argument, most eloquently laid out by John Birt and Peter Jay in *The Times*, was that the prevalence of images on television (and thus, though they didn't say it, narrative journalism) was somehow vulgar or inappropriate, a legacy of the roots of television news in tabloid journalism or its offshoot, documentaries. There was 'a bias against understanding' in television, which threatened the rest of the media, like a contagion. Nowadays television is even more anchored than it was within the idiom of story-telling. Documentaries have contributed to this tendency. They have also enthroned narrative, for better or worse, within a wider culture.

Unlike print stories or non-fiction books, or indeed novels, documentaries supply the frisson of the real. Only live coverage of sporting events or atrocities can compete with them. And the range of stories to be found in documentaries is dazzlingly wide. There are few subjects indeed – medical, political, scientific, whatever – that can't be, or haven't been, given documentary treatment.

---

51   In Europe cinema documentary attendance is much smaller; see Appendix 2. But *Fahrenheit 9/11* made £6.5 million and *Touching the Void*, the most successful British documentary film in recent years, a respectable £2.6 million.

Stories are also immersive. You get into them, and you get out again. The best recent documentaries are instantly immersive, hard to leave.

Is there a cultural loss when one focuses so exclusively on the properties of stories? Only if you believe that the human brain, in isolation or in aggregate, can only interpret significant aspects of reality in one way at a time. This would seem improbable, to say the least. Meanwhile I enjoy reports from people who have found themselves in hotel rooms, somewhere in the world, and who came across a documentary story, often half way through the action, and who stayed. *A Cry from the Grave* (1999) tells the story, in exhaustive detail, of the Srebrenica massacre, in which more than 7,000 Bosnian Muslims died. There have been accounts of this event, the worst postwar killing in Europe, in books, legal documents, individual testimonies. Leslie Woodhead's film was shown in many places – at the United Nations, at The Hague, where it was used in court testimony, in Belgrade where it was among the first accounts of the massacre made available to the Serb public. Millions have sat through this scrupulous, often gruelling and disheartening account of human wickedness and incompetence. But I also received an email from a woman who had been tidying up her children's toys when the film was shown on BBC2. She was surprised to find herself sitting on a bed in front of the television set, three-quarters of an hour later, still holding the toys.

One Day in September (1999), Kevin Macdonald's retelling of the 1972 massacre of Israeli athletes at the Munich Olympic Games, similarly restricted itself to an hour-by-hour account of what happened. By design there was no attempt to place the Black September terrorists in a larger context – on the grounds that this could be done in other films less purely focused on the story of the 24 hours, and that those interested could go elsewhere for a history of Palestinian activism. Writing in the *Guardian*, Edward Said criticised this perspective.[52] Said's point of view is primarily political, but he also displays the habitual aversion of print people towards the alleged oversimplification of narrative film. Similar tart observations were made by the poet Tom Paulin about *One Day in September* when speaking on the BBC. My own objections to the position of Paulin and Said come from the degree to which they, and those who agree with them, are so reluctant to admit the real potential of film. Instead of complaining about the impact of documentary films, it might be better to consider what they do so well. And they describe events very vividly. They can also be used to cast doubt on what appear to be familiar narratives. It took a long time for documentaries to emerge from the either/or constraints of traditional factual programming, but film-makers are now happier with ambiguity. You can cast doubt on a story while you tell it nowadays. And you

---

52   Said's piece appeared on Saturday 20 May 2000. A rebuttal letter by Kevin Macdonald was printed the following week.

can certainly use multiple, shifting points of view in order to wheel audiences around the perimeters of a subject, as good print journalists have always done.

Many of the best recent documentary films possess this same, wholly gripping quality of borderline obsession combined with uncertainty. These qualities are present in *Hoop Dreams*, in the struggles to become basketball stars of William Gates and Arthur. They dominate Leon Gast's Oscar-winning *When We Were Kings* (1996), which recreates Muhammad Ali's 'rumble in the jungle'. And they recur in Terry Zwigoff's *Crumb* (1994), which starts like a caper, bumps into the reality of Crumb's artistic abilities, and ends as a study of a family pathology from which Crumb has escaped via his art. Maybe they can be seen, too, in *Wanted and Desired* (2008), Marina Zenovic's study of Roman Polanski's 1977 Los Angeles legal entanglements following the rape of a minor. What Polanski did is here told clearly enough, in brutal detail; so too is his erratic treatment at the hands of a judge who at times appears to be deranged. But the ultimate effect of the film is unsettling, and the question of whether and how Polanski might additionally have been punished is left wholly open.[53] There is no suggestion that the views of French intellectuals, many of whom believed that Polanski, because of his great talent, should have been permitted to do what he wanted, are worth taking seriously.

Uncertainty of a different kind permeates Robert Stone's *Guerilla* (2003), which recreates the kidnapping and brief bank robber career of the heiress Patty Hearst. The Hearst story is familiar enough, certainly to anyone over 50, but here the narrative is rebuilt out of a combination of archive (culled from rubbish tips, sometimes, when it was thrown out by local Californian stations) and often highly misleading recollections. The absence of Hearst from the film adds to the eerie, almost ghostly quality of mid-1970s California evoked here. The deeper you get, Patty's story seems to tell us, the more uncertain it all becomes. And the same radical unsettlement pervades the recent *Armadillo* (2010), a film that follows young Danish soldiers in Afghanistan, much criticised for the way it appears to exclude anything else of the war in order to focus on its panicky, baffled subjects. Do these young Danes needlessly kill the few Taleban they ultimately find? Director Janus Metz Pedersen leaves us to decide. Why would we wish anything otherwise?

Campaigners

The most successful agitprop film of recent years was Al Gore's *An Inconvenient Truth* (2006), which took $49 million at the box office throughout the world, won two Oscars, and finally restored Gore to public life. Stylistically, Davis

---

53   Some critics suggested that the film was overly sympathetic to Polanski. In my view this was because the director Marina Zenovic didn't go out of her way to condemn Polanski. In fact the film says very clearly that Polanski was guilty. The question of whether he should have been imprisoned, or what might have been a suitable punishment, is left to the participants, all of whom have divergent views on the matter.

Guggenheim's film was neither original nor executed with great flair – it was a lecture, filmed on separate occasions, in which Gore crossed the stage to emphasise the points he was making, and it should maybe be seen as a predecessor of the TED lectures, now posted online – but it was nonetheless highly effective. Gore presented what he considered to be the facts surrounding global warming with flair, and in a spirit of desperate cheerfulness. He was impressive because (as the film reminded viewers, with sequences of its protagonist getting on and off planes) he had taken the trouble to find out about climate change. This wasn't a cause strategically espoused but a lifelong concern, and Gore's conclusions went way beyond the sonorous expressions of concern we have come to expect from politicians and newscasters:

> *Each one of us is a cause of global warming, but each one*
> *of us can make choices to change that with the things we*
> *buy, the electricity we use, the cars we drive; we can make*
> *choices to bring our individual carbon emissions to zero.*
> *The solutions are in our hands, we just have to have the*
> *determination to make it happen. We have everything that*
> *we need to reduce carbon emissions, everything but political*
> *will. But in America, the will to act is a renewable resource.*

It would appear, too, that the appeal was effective. Of viewers who claimed to have seen *An Inconvenient Truth,* 66% said the film had 'changed their mind' about global warming and 89% said watching the movie made them more aware of the problem. Three out of four viewers said they changed some of their habits as a result of seeing the film. The film appears to have offended those who resented the rehabilitation of Al Gore, or didn't take global warning seriously. George Bush said he hadn't seen the film. Oklahoma Republican Senator Jim Inhofe said he didn't plan to see the film (which he appeared in). Bizarrely he compared the film to *Mein Kampf:* 'If you say the same lie over and over again, and particularly if you have the media's support, people will believe it.' In Britain, as a consequence of a court case brought by Stewart Dimmock, a lorry driver and activist, the film was found to contain nine 'errors' – i.e. *instances,* legally defined, where Gore was thought to depart from mainstream scientific views. But the judge didn't condemn the film, suggesting that Gore had throughout his argument done his best to be accurate, and declined to deny the film access to schools, as the plaintiffs had demanded.[54]

There have been many less successful films in the campaigning idiom. Those who still think that good intentions can be enough should witness

54   Gore's conclusion, the response of Inhofe, and an account of the Dimmock case are to be found in the Wikipedia entry describing *An Inconvenient Truth.*

Leonardo di Caprio narrating *The Eleventh Hour* (2007). It would seem, not wholly surprisingly, that people won't go to cinemas to be hectored and, in many instances, don't want to see such material on television. So maybe the internet rather than the multiplex is the best place for overt campaigning. One exception, however, is Franny Armstrong's *Age of Stupid* (2009). Armstrong was once a drummer with indie pop group The Band of Holy Joy. In 2005 she made a film about the libel suit brought by McDonalds against two activists. But Armstrong insists that she doesn't only address the converted. In *The Age of Stupid*, with the help of an actor, the late Pete Postlethwaite, she created an abandoned spacecraft on which the last inhabitant of earth is able to go back through contemporary archive film, riffling through our present in order to discover why humanity allowed its precious habitat to be destroyed. Clunky, consciously unjournalistic, daring in its reluctance to be bound by any sense of what is credible, and what isn't, the film is nonetheless persuasive, and in its own special way, shocking, as if the young H. G. Wells had come back with a cheap camera and a low budget.[55]

Everything personal

In 1990, the BBC launched a series of video diaries. Shot with the latest light-weight cameras (they would seem bulky now) the films were tightly supervised. Many depicted personal quests of the film-makers, and these were expressed in the common contemporary idiom of self-realisation drawn from therapy. Victimhood was a common theme. However, *The Man Who Loved Gary Lineker* was altogether different. This was a day-by-day account by an Albanian doctor, who tended his patients as best he could in circumstances of Communist era poverty. As leisure, all he could find were the soccer matches beamed faintly to Albania from Italian television.

As one might expect, documentary authorship was given a personal slant, most of all in the US with its therapeutic culture of self-disclosure. Alan Berliner's *Nobody's Business* (1996) is a candid memoir of a grumpy Jewish father unable to communicate with his son and afflicted by deafness. Berliner is able to hide or mitigate a certain degree of self-absorption by recourse to an impersonal, highly organised editing style, and the viewer is able to forget that Berliner's true subject is himself. As he explains on his own website, alluding to another film *Wide Awake*, describing his own insomnia:[56]

---

55   *McLibel* was successfully shown on television throughout the world. *No Pressure* (2010), a short devised by Armstrong with the screenwriter Richard Curtis, depicted people being blown up at a touch of a button when they were asked to join the 10:10 ecological campaign and refused. It was withdrawn following protests. Armstrong first used the new method of crowd funding for *The Age of Stupid*, and she created the carbon reduction campaign 10:10.
56   Alanberliner.com.

*Berliner uses both metaphor and candid first-person
observations to illuminate how an obsessive mind that won't
shut down at night leaves him feeling 'jet lagged in his own
time zone.' Incorporating hundreds of archival film clips,
consultations with sleep specialists, an overnight stay at a
sleep lab, conversations with family members, home movies
and dream visualizations – all woven together by a strikingly
dynamic sound design – WIDE AWAKE is a cinematically
innovative film that pushes at the borders of documentary film.*

Another diarist is Jennifer Fox, whose *Flying* (2008) is a six-hour experiment in feminist autobiography. Fox the film-maker jets around the world from New York to Johannesburg, to rural Pakistan and India. In remote places she investigates the condition of women, while back in Manhattan she attempts to have a child, and look after sick friends. Fox is a gifted and compassionate observer, and the films come into their own as a family history, with the touchingly described death of her much-loved grandmother. Such scenes sit uneasily with the quizzing of Indian peasants about masturbation, though the contrast may tell us more than Fox imagines about the world of difference between rich and poor lives in the contemporary world.

Another first-person film is *My Architect* (2003), in which the film-maker Nathaniel Kahn goes in search of his father Louis Kahn. Kahn senior was one of the least conventional architects of the 20th century, designing, among other wonders, a boat from which symphonic music could be played and the parliamentary buildings of Bangladesh, at that time one of the poorest countries in the world. But Kahn's life wasn't as ordered as his ingenious buildings. After his sudden death, in transit and in a washroom of New York's Penn Station, his son unearths three separate families each claiming something of Kahn's life. In the end the sheer eccentricity of Kahn senior combines with his architectural genius to make his odd domestic arrangements seem quite natural, and one can begin to realise how much effort to reach this conclusion was required of his tolerant and loving son.

More reticent, indirect in an English way, is Luke Holland's *A Very English Village*. Holland, an urban-seeming intellectual, lives in Ditchling, a picture-postcard Sussex village, and his account of its inhabitants doubles as an exploration of his own borderline-rapturous, ironical discovery of English semi-rural eccentricity. Filmed at the beginning of the century, Holland's films hark back to the many 1930s attempts made by Orwell and his contemporaries to discover what it means to be truly English.

Do filmed autobiographies have a future? Anyone can now post whatever they wish to say about themselves, courtesy of YouTube. But the autobiographical impulse isn't invariably a pretext for good films, and it is possible to wonder how interesting such experiments will soon seem. In *We Live in Public* (2009), Ondi Timoner describes the brief career of Josh Harris who created a community in downtown Manhattan in which participants lived in public via the internet. Harris placed his own life online, 24 hours a day, with what Timoner describes as bizarrely catastrophic results when the collective online community disintegrated, and Harris's girlfriend, somewhat predictably, left him. Taken as a whole, confessional filming in the internet age seems irritating, easy to parody. It may be harder to give an account of yourself on camera than it is in print, though to look at the efforts of many exponents of the genre, one wouldn't conclude that many are aware of the problems.

Super-reporters

Reportage has been altered by the pervasive, uncontroversial use of the first person; and it is also possible to think of many films that slip in and out of the first person without excessive fuss. Instances of this can be found in the work of Nick Broomfield, most of all *The Leader, his Driver and the Driver's Wife* (1990), in which he stalks Eugene Terreblanche, a dementedly driven, self-important Afrikaner white supremacist, and the two films Broomfield made about the convicted serial killer Aileen Wuornos (1993 and 2003). Broomfield's brass, self-deprecation, and unfeigned curiosity allow him to intervene in the story he's telling, but the films, despite an insistent presence, with trademark drawl and sound boom, don't usually appear to be about himself. In Britain a Broomfield school of social observation now exists, featuring (usually male and borderline scruffy) talents such as Louis Theroux and Sean McAllister. Previously, such reporters would have appeared as ordinary television presenters, but their presence can now be experienced differently, as diarists and authors as well as reporters. The same transformation occurs in Morgan Spurlock's best film, *Super Size Me* (2004) filmed over 30 days during which he eats only food from McDonalds, gorging himself three times a day with prime (and sublimely unhealthy) offerings. By consuming 5,000 kcal (the equivalent of 9.26 Big Macs) per day, Spurlock gained 24½ lbs, a 13% body mass increase, leading to a cholesterol level of 230. It took him 14 months to lose the weight gained from this experiment.

The most persistent, successful reporter-author is, of course, Michael Moore. In his many box office successes the bulky Moore assails exponents of free market capitalism in a series of gags, or entraps them with shrewd interviews. The films are perfunctorily put together, which gives them an air of improvised journalism, though the effects are, as one might expect, highly calculated. No one should complain about Moore's political stance, which is overtly expressed. He's polemical, leftish, anti-authoritarian, and the onscreen truculence enables him to avoid the self-righteousness of much left-wing commentary: Moore's commentaries eschew even-handedness as much as those of Glenn Beck. In *Bowling for Columbine*, an otherwise excellent investigation into gun ownership, his attempts to confront a Charlton Heston suffering from Alzheimer's disease seem cruel, as well as patronising. Moore's journalistic standards are slippery and at times non-existent. In *Fahrenheit 9/11* he characterised Saddam Hussein's Iraq as a paradise rudely destroyed by America. *Sicko* contains what seems to Brits to be a ridiculous over-praising of the NHS and the Cuban medical system. Moore's first film *Roger and Me* (1989) describes the fate of Flint, Michigan, in which he grew up, after the GM plant closed. But the plot consists of Moore's unsuccessful attempts to interview Roger Smith, the boss of General Motors, and Moore, it seems, did actually get to interview Smith.[57]

It would nonetheless be wrong to make too much of Moore's numerous elisions and partial truths, because he has never claimed to be a reporter. His job, as he has stated often, is to entertain. Moore tells his audiences they mustn't believe in anything they are told by politicians or corporations. He made possible the clever satire of media in Jon Stewart's *Daily Show*. An autobiography tells how unpopular Michael Moore's views were. In the post-9/11 hysteria Moore's driveway was filled with excrement and he was the recipient of numerous threats. After he was attacked in the street he was obliged to hire 24-hour guards, some of them ex Navy Seals. Prior to making *Fahrenheit 9/11* it would seem that he contemplated abandoning documentary film, on the grounds that it was too dangerous.[58] In a different way, therefore, Moore has proved to be almost as influential as the output of Fox News. And that, whatever you think of his film-making style, is a signal achievement.

Witness(ing)

In 2008 I was driven around the Palestine West Bank in an armoured jeep. My guide wanted to show me the sheer extent of the means used by the Israeli army to separate settler communities from the Palestinian Arabs surrounding them. He had given small cameras to the Arabs, granting them the capability of recording the attacks to which they were subject. Since the cameras had arrived, he pointed out, the number of aggressions had diminished.[59] In this small, functional way, we could learn to use media in a radically different style.

The historian Jean Seaton has suggested that, beginning with the Balkan wars of the 1990s, images displaced written accounts as a primary source. 'News is *The Guardian* and *The Sun*,' she says. 'It is also Goya, George Eliot and

---

57   Rick Caine and Debbie Melnyk's film, *Manufacturing Dissent* (2007). Moore hasn't ever explained this discrepancy, suggesting his encounter with Smith wasn't a 'real' interview. If it was, Moore suggests, somewhat disingenuously, GM would have gone after him.
58   *Here Comes Trouble Stories from my Life* (Penguin, 2011), quoted in *Guardian*, G2, 8 Sept. 2011.
59   The Israeli foundation B'Tselem hands out the cameras, collecting the footage. Records of abuse are kept and handed over to the police and courts. They have led to cases being brought in Israeli courts.

George Orwell. News is about observation and imagination, not mechanics.[60] But news has also become what anyone who happens to be there can record. News indeed has ceased to be the exclusive property of professionals. Amateur footage gave the world the celebrated Zapruder tapes, in which JFK's death is recorded, back in the 1960s. It has now become possible for the first time to tell contemporary stories in great detail, through the use of much larger archives, and material shot casually.

Among those exploring the possibilities of archive, the work of Norma Percy and Brian Lapping stands out. They began their careers working for the Granada Television that sustained *World in Action*. Percy and Lapping, however, aren't investigative journalists of a conventional sort. 'We like to be in the corridors of power,' Lapping says.[61] By previewing their interviewees, cross-checking testimony, and reinterviewing when necessary, they are able to build up astonishingly detailed accounts of political events. They insist on the most rigorous impartiality, and it is this quality that secures their access to the powerful. A Lapping-Percy film is sometimes a bit like a good political science seminar, but there can be drama, too. *The Death of Yugoslavia* (1995), their six-part series chronicling the Balkan wars of the 1990s, attains a level of factual detail not habitually seen in a documentary film. It remains surprising just how much of the action was recorded, often by the official cameramen of each nation. But the twists and turns of intrigue prove to be surprisingly engaging. It's also evident when the participants are telling the truth, even in Serbo-Croat, and when they are merely rehashing their own roles for presumed effect.[62]

From the 1990s onwards, the old well-trodden path of factual documentaries bifurcated, and split again. Suddenly there were many ways of making a film about contemporary reality. One could adopt a polemical approach, or one could construct out of the immediate past a narrative that eschewed interpretation, focusing on the recreation of events in a highly dramatic style. Among the polemics, *The Trials of Henry Kissinger* (2002) by Alex Gibney and Eugene Jarecki, and *Why We Fight* (2005) by Eugene Jarecki, assail big moments of our time indirectly, tempering denunciation with curiosity. Jarecki's *Reagan* (2011) is compulsively revealing about its mysteriously bland and shallow subject. Alex Gibney's *Enron: The Smartest Guys in the Room* (2005) and his Oscar-winning *Taxi to the Dark Side* (2007) are sleekly edited investigations built around revelations of character and motivation as well as fact. Gibney displays much well-grounded indignation in relation to corporate malfeasance, but his action-packed narratives stave off weariness, sustaining audience interest. Another successful piece of documentary muck-

---

60   Jean Seaton, *Carnage and the Media: The Making and Breaking of News about Violence* (Penguin, 2005), 296.
61   Author's interview.
62   Other series by Lapping and Percy include *Israel and the Arabs* (2005) and *Iran and the West* (2009).

raking is Charles Ferguson's assault on Wall Street, *Inside Job* (2010). By its author's admission this is an attempt to indict not just individuals but a style of financial capitalism, too. Structured like an essay, narrated by a sober-sides Matt Damon, the film moves from one egregious abuse to another. Chapter by chapter, with the tone of a formal indictment, *Inside Job* is an impressive piece of public film-making, claiming as it does to speak not just for individual victims of fraud but for the entire American people, on whom, Ferguson is certain, a giant swindle was perpetrated. It takes a while for one to appreciate how just how one-sided and unyielding is Ferguson's analysis. He was helped along in his efforts, however, by the refusal of major players to collaborate. Are these bosses as guilty as Ferguson implies? Certainly the many millions who saw this Oscar-winning film must have concluded that yes, they were. And with Ferguson's film, documentary film attained a political importance never seen before.

The television bubble

Television is for the most part without perceptible style. The narratives of television come concealed behind a bland, undifferentiated flow of images. Film-makers can choose to allow themselves to drown in the flow, or they can attempt to use the non-idiom of television for subversive purposes. Adam Curtis has developed his own idiosyncratic approach both to the use of archive film and the entire idea of reporting. Curtis trained as a psychologist, and his films make a point of always following the route not taken by conventional mass media narratives; his real subject is the difficulty we have in knowing anything at all. In *The Century of the Self* (2002) he looked at the private as well the public lies of the 20th century. *The Power of Nightmares* (2004) hacked into Islamism and the Neo-cons not from the usual contemporary perspective of Bush's War of Terror, but from deep within the history of ideas. In a donnish, laid-back way, it was gripping even when not wholly convincing. Curtis's latest series *All Watched Over by Loving Machines* (2011) does much the same thing, with similar provocative effects, setting the overweening utopian pretensions of the internet against darker warnings about the destructive power of machines, and the illusions surrounding their beneficence.

Curtis has acquired the knack of constructing sequences out of apparently disconnected images, thus avoiding the clichéd illustrative style of television. As he explains, he began by rooting around in discarded BBC footage.

> '*That kind of footage shows just how dull I can be,*' he admits,
> a little glumly. '*The BBC has an archive of all these tapes
> where they have just dumped all the news items they have
> ever shown. One tape for every three months. So what you
> get is this odd collage, an accidental treasure trove. You sit in*

a darkened room, watch all these little news moments, and look for connections.[63]

It's a mistake to subject Curtis's films to extensive factual tests, and one gets nowhere by picking holes in his arguments. They give an impression of how things might be if one looked at them in a slightly different way. But there's no ignoring the Curtis obsession with reality. If only we understood, he seems to say – politicians most of all, but the rest of us, too, since we collude in the circulation of half-truths through our mistaken attachment to politicians – we might be better off. Still, we won't understand. Even if we do, just a little, it won't always be clear to us that we do. So we can remain in the dark, or watch his films.

Animate

In 1982, Ari Folman was a 19-year-old infantry soldier in the Israel Defense Forces, and he took part in the Lebanon War. He didn't remember anything, but in 2006 a conversation with a friend who still had nightmares set him dreaming horrors from his own past. Folman's memories led him to make *Waltz with Bashir* (2008), a dark feature-length animated film in which the interviews are genuine, but the animation displays a high degree of artistry, never pretending to reflect literally the real events it depicts. The film ends with the animation dissolving into real – and truly horrifying – footage of the Sabra and Chatila massacre. Folman doesn't give an overview of the war, and he certainly doesn't explain how the massacre was perpetrated, or what was the exact role of the IDF. He wants to tell his own story, and the animation allows him to show how he (and much of the rest of Israel) has blocked off what happened, suppressing reality until it becomes just another narrative among many. In the wake of Folman's inspired experiment, however, film-makers have developed an addiction to animation, and one can see how attractive the method can seem as a means of supplying images when these aren't available. Yet sliding in and out of real images creates a degree of distance, ultimately diminishing the subject.

The myth of truth

'Cinema, like poetry, is inherently able to present a number of dimensions much deeper than the level of the so-called truth that we find in cinéma verité and even reality itself,' says Werner Herzog. 'I truly hope to be one of those who finally bury cinéma verité for good.'[64] Herzog's Ballardesque fictions are heavily indebted to documentary, filmed in uncomfortable places with

---

63 *Observer*, 17 Feb. 2010.
64 *Herzog on Herzog*, ed. Paul Cronin (Faber & Faber, 2002), 239.

a brilliantly wayward attention to the retention of rough edges. Herzog has always insisted that his many, wonderful documentaries are shaped in much the same way. It would be folly to restrict oneself, Herzog believes, to the literal annotation of the world when so much more can be done. But Herzog, despite the admiration for artifice, has his own poorly camouflaged passion for truth. In film after film he attacks head on what he conceives to be the most important lie told by humans about themselves or the world that they inhabit – that it was made for them, that what we call nature or referred to as human civilisation is in any way pleasant or accommodating.

Little Dieter Needs to Fly (1997) tells the story of Dieter Dengler, who grew up in a wartime German village over which American planes flew at near ground-level. Like Jim, in Ballard's *Empire of the Sun*, Dieter became obsessed by the possibility of flight. He was one of the few foreigners able to sign up, once he was naturalised, as a pilot in the US air force and then, in order to fly combat missions, joined the US Navy. Shot down over Laos, he was captured by Pathet Lao guerrillas, turned over to North Vietnamese soldiers and tortured; but he escaped. Herzog returned to this story in *Rescue Dawn* (2007), replaying it with actors; but it is the middle-aged, deeply damaged Dengler who best recreates his own story. *Little Dieter Needs to Fly* is built out of recreations, and one can see that these have been staged. Often indeed one can witness Herzog in the overweening style of Lanzmann constraining the hapless Dengler to revisit his own horrors. Nonetheless, the film does attain Dengler's truth about himself. It never appears in the least contrived, and this a tribute to Herzog's great artfulness.

In recent years Herzog's shamanic properties have come to the fore in a series of reportorial films in which he appears as a protagonist, sounding like a cross between Nietzsche and Alan Whicker. His most remarkable recent film, *Grizzly Man* (2005), balances contempt for the sentimental attachment to bears of the ill-fated Timothy Treadwell with pity for the fate that befell him, when the creatures he claimed to love, indifferent to his interest, turned on him. Herzog declines to let us hear the dying bear-lover's screams, and one can feel oddly exhilarated as well as relieved by his solicitousness – because Herzog, after half a lifetime of struggle, has finally been able to accommodate his obsessions with pain and death within a highly shaped narrative.

Reality shows

So-called 'reality television' is an opportunistically conceived offshoot of documentary in which the 'real' element has been captured for television, artificially reconfigured. It's a way of selling the notion of reality, of making the habitual less unexciting. Contrary to the views of many television executives, reality shows aren't in competition with documentaries. They may satisfy some of the same hungers as documentaries, but they do so in different ways.

Meanwhile film-makers have begun to examine the psychological reach of contemporary media. The sheer range of ways in which truth can now be tampered with has opened new possibilities for film-makers. Andrew Jarecki's *Capturing the Friedmans* (2003) opened up the possibility of making films in which the final effect isn't any certainty whatsoever but a suspended state of unease. Were Arnold and Jessie Friedman, suburban father and son, really guilty of child abuse? They pled guilty, and were convicted; but both cast doubt on their own testimony. The film insists that we cannot really know what happened, even as it sets out to chronicle the Friedman story exhaustively. Earlier films might have offered reasons for not coming to any firm conclusions, but Andrew Jarecki leaves us with the nagging sense that much of life can be captured but never fully known.

Catfish (2010, also produced by Andrew Jarecki) tells us how it is possible to invent a life via social networks. Its heroine's creation of a glamorous, high-performing family to atone for the dismal circumstances in which she finds herself, poor and with two disabled children, is never wholly convincing, even to herself. But it provides the basis for a quest for reality on the part of two media-savvy New Yorkers. Whether the film is wholly truthful has been a subject of debate, but when you watch *Catfish* this doesn't seem to matter much. Instead, with much skill, just enough sympathy, and a shrewd assessment of where contemporary mores are headed, we're directed to the saving possibilities of fibs. This could be you. You may have such an appalling life that lying is the only way out. And, in any case, by coming clean, you fulfil traditional Hollywood expectations of a redemptive ending in which truth appears to triumph over the fantasies now available to everyone courtesy of social media.

Lying, too, albeit of a very different kind, is the subject of Errol Morris's *Tabloid* (2010), which tells the story of Joyce McKinney, sometime prom queen, dog cloner, and the centre of a long-forgotten tabloid sex caper of the 1970s known as The Case of the Manacled Mormon. McKinney may or may not have tied a Mormon to a bed for sex romps in a Dorset 'rural love cottage'. Whether she did or not isn't really the subject of the film. Morris's films touch invariably on the subject of misapprehension – mistaken identities, photographs that give a highly partial version of reality, human beings (such as Robert McNamara in *Fog of War*) who strive less than successfully, often out of a deep degree of self-delusion, never quite to give a full account of themselves. Here he's interested in the way in which tabloids come to stand in for the truth. We may think we can tell the truth about the events around us, but that may prove to be a comfortable illusion. It would be more accurate to say that we could tell the truth if we weren't ourselves so enveloped by half-truth and outright lies. But why are the lies so seductive? Out of a long-forgotten minor tabloid scandal, Morris has woven his own, wholly convincing account of human collusion in the subversion of reality. I watched Morris's film during the week when Murdoch's tabloid vision of politics in Britain was finally called to account. It seemed both an exercise in nostalgia, and a warning – this is what happens if you take fictions too seriously, at the very least you become a prisoner of them. You may in time come to be overcome by their power, as was the case with the British political class, held in thrall for so long by the dark reach, powerful but illusory, of the Murdoch Empire.

Global

You can now shoot and edit a film anywhere in the world, and show it on YouTube. Documentary film-makers have indeed become a world community. But there is no global style of film-making. (There is of course the Discovery Channel, packed with commentary and animal close-ups, and there are the devices of news reporting; but these can't be defined as a style.) Instead, film-makers are engaged in their own separate, often impassioned, and hazardous quests to make sense of the world. In many parts of the world, state broadcasters exercise a monopoly, and here film-makers are reliant exclusively on outside support. Zhao Liang's *Petition* (2009), which took ten years to make, chronicles the non-functioning of the only court in China to which petitioners can take complaints of corruption of public officials. The court, which dates from Mandarin times, sits in secret and in many instances may take eight or ten years to pass judgment. It becomes rapidly evident that this isn't a real commitment to justice, and that the authorities tolerate its existence merely so that they can say it is there. Meanwhile petitioners, having come to Beijing, live in a shanty town around the court office called Petition City, and this is pulled down. Zhao Liang's film has never been shown in Beijing.[65]

It has been possible, however, to show a number of Chinese films in the West made without sanction of the authorities. In some instances the films have later found an appreciative though still 'unofficial' audience in China. As an example, consider the fate of *To Live is Better than to Die* (2002). Weijun Chen was a producer at the state Wuhan television service when he became aware of the hitherto unreported effects of contaminated needles, which had resulted in many villagers who sold blood becoming HIV positive. He filmed the fate of the Ma family, and he was present when the mother and baby son began to exhibit the symptoms of AIDS, dying soon after. How did this affect the father and the daughter? They survived, and the father found another wife whose own husband had died of AIDS. But the recompense offered was pitifully small, and it was evident that the authorities wished to keep all evidence of the epidemic from the public eye. Sent to the Sundance Festival,

---

65   See *New York Times*, 14 Aug. 2011, for an illuminating account of Zhao Liang's relations with the Chinese authorities, including official efforts to sponsor his next film.

the film was shown in the West, where it won a number of prizes. It then became required viewing for Communist officials. Apparently these unofficial showings led to a more generous attitude to the victims of official carelessness, though it could not be aired on television. In a circuitous fashion the film thus had a considerable impact.

In Russia, documentaries if deemed offensive are removed from the internet; Russian networks do not show documentaries, indeed they do not screen independent material. Until the arrival on the scene of Al-Jazeera, there were no independent documentaries in the Arab world. In India, where commercial television now dominates the market, it is hard to find documentaries. It remains extremely difficult to make documentaries if you come from a poor country or a repressive culture. It's worse than trying to be a journalist in a country without newspapers – because, despite so many advances in technology, documentary films are more expensive to create and harder to distribute. But a rudimentary system for showing documentaries globally exists. Only two decades ago films about what were thought of as remote parts of the world were made by visiting Europeans or North Americans whose efforts, no matter how serious, often displayed an element of lofty condescension. All this has changed now. In *Bus 174* (2002) José Padilha was able to uncover the story of Sandro do Nascimento, who kept a number of passengers hostage for some hours while police attempted to negotiate with him, finally killing him after they had stormed the bus. The hi-jacking was carried live on Brazilian television, but no one knew anything about the perpetrator. Thanks to Padilha we know that he was young, that his mother was a prostitute, that he went through the Rio orphanage system, that he was addicted to glue, unstable, and that an aunt had tried unsuccessfully to save him from the streets where he lived rough. In official language he would be seen as a member of the underclass, but that is not how he appears in Padilha's wrenchingly eloquent film.

Or consider, finally, the story of the 20-year-old trainee chef Paco Larraniega, arrested in the Philippines in 1997 for the murder of two young women that he didn't commit. He was found guilty, spent years on Death Row, and 14 years later he's still in prison, now in Spain. *Give Up Tomorrow* (2011), which tells the story of Paco's frustrated struggle to obtain justice, has become part of the legal campaign to free him. The film has had a greater impact than any piece of written journalism. It has helped create a global campaign around his fate. Efforts such as this aren't yet routine, and they aren't integrated within a system by which films such as this may be regularly screened for global audiences. But it is possible to hope that they soon will be.

# 5.	Future Documentaries: investing to save civilisation

Documentaries are too expensive to be produced like pamphlets, or their contemporary equivalent, blogs. They don't make a lot of money, so the complex percentage-based investments governing feature films don't really apply to them. In parallel with the narrative recounting of how documentaries evolved runs the secondary hand-to-mouth story of their funding. For a long time they relied on private finance until this gave way to state patronage and, later, to the generosity of public broadcasters. But nowadays most documentaries are funded from a variety of sources, private and public, corporate and philanthropic. A giveaway is the increasingly complicated set of euphemisms used to acknowledge the provenance of each film. Another would be the long lists of patrons.

But it is hard not to conclude that while more films are being made each year, budgets are falling. The economics of documentary production aren't visibly improving. It takes longer to fund a production, and there are more film-makers each year. Malthus-style, film-makers are becoming poorer. The process of funding documentary films is laborious and, to outsiders, hard to comprehend. It seems a miracle that any film gets made.

How can the funding of documentaries be improved? How will they be shown in the future? Can they survive and thrive in the circumstances of online digital distribution? I think they can and will survive, and propose to show how. But first it is necessary to acquire some knowledge of documentary film funding. The best way to enter the strange, upside-down world of documentary finance is through pitches.

Each year, and in many less than glamorous places, television executives, producers, documentary directors, and representatives of various foundations and documentary funds meet to evaluate projects. Ideas are publicly pitched and argued over. With due delays, and when the participants have conferred with other executives at home, budgets can be assembled, more often than not small package by package. Why does it take so long to find the money? Do the best projects survive the process of being pitched? No one ever thought of publicly pitching a half-written piece of journalism. No one personally felt obliged to take to market a half-written play, a novel that exists primarily in the author's head, a non-fiction book or piece of journalism the success of which depends on a degree of collaboration that hasn't yet been achieved, or a screenplay consisting of a number of scenes as yet not worked out. And what happens to those who are bad at self-presentation? They can't survive.

And yet these events are surprisingly popular, drawing an audience comprised of observers and fans. They are reasonably effective. The most venerable, which takes place each November in Amsterdam,[66] was started 15 years ago. In its first years the IDFA Forum was a place where ideas were discussed. People argued about the kind of documentaries that should be shown on television and in cinemas. Arguments were often acrimonious, pitting different tendencies and schools against each other.

Over the years presentations became slicker. Inevitably projects drew closer to the mainstream, or in time, when people saw what worked and what didn't, became part of their own mainstream. Funding documentaries in this way acquired its own momentum to go with the ritual. Broadcasters would now put up small sums of money in order to bring a new project to market. The sponsors of a project acquired partners. With three or more partners, they could start production. Smaller broadcasters could then buy into the production. Having financed the film, often at a modest level, producers were now free to earn additional money from distributors by selling their films worldwide.

Those prepared to spend time raising money in this way were often young, unknown, unfussy.[67] It suddenly became possible to finance many films which would never have seen the light of day. On the minus side, funding was never reliable. Making documentaries remained a marginal, risky endeavour. And documentaries continued to depend, overwhelmingly, on the patronage of public broadcasters. For a long time, indeed, they were the only funders of documentaries. Even within public broadcasters, among those who counted, documentaries were not excessively valued. They didn't reliably secure ratings. Many television executives weren't specially interested in documentaries, though they were too polite to say so. They much preferred the new format

66   The forum is organised by IDFA, the Amsterdam documentary festival. It lasts for three days and some 40 projects are discussed. It is funded by the European Union media fund, and the City of Amsterdam, among others, and IDFA estimates than in any one year more than €10 million of deals are done. Similar events now take place throughout the world, in Asia, Africa, and Latin America.

67   Influential in helping along such projects is the EU Media Fund for documentaries. Part of an ambitious attempt to shore up European cinema by subsidising distribution, this offers up to 20% of a budget if the producer can supply more than four European broadcasters willing to show the film. The scheme is neutral, in the sense that the subject of the film isn't relevant – even films critical of the EU itself receive support – and, within the limits imposed by a relatively small budget, very effective.

shows when they weren't spending money on increasingly costly sports rights.[68]

Although budgets have shrunk, or at best remained static, many factors have contrived to hide this. It has become easier to make films cheaply, with the low cost of stock and equipment, and producers have become good at this. But there must come a time when the decline in ambition is apparent. Look at the catalogues issued before each trade fair, or the schedules of any digital channel in Western Europe. You might be forgiven for failing to discern any lack of funding or interest in documentaries. But poverty is often visible on the screen – poor archive, over-reliance on the staple of talking heads, low or non-existent standards of journalism, themes and facts stretched to cover the vast empty spaces required each day. Because television by and large has less money, and executives delay decisions, the time taken to raise money for a project has doubled and doubled again. Projects with a short life, or a niche interest, even those closest to the traditional interests of public broadcasters, are harder and harder to fund.

Meanwhile there are numerous film funds and other quangos set up to encourage films. France's venerable CNC (Centre Nationale Cinématographique) is based on cinema receipts, from which an expectation of future revenues can be taken, and a grant made available. The CNC observes editorial neutrality, but it favours existing producers of fictions, who can claim the largest sums. Others (this was the German model, extended to Scotland) distribute largesse according to regional content, or because the producer came from the region. The most durable, legitimate-sounding funds are set up to foster national cultures. In Canada, working in French as well as English and giving expression to indigenous voices, the equally venerable National Film Board (set up according to the recommendations of John Grierson and still, after all these years, bearing his stamp) represents the most complex system of non-broadcast funding. Canadian producers view the Board with a mixture of affection and exasperation. It places chosen film-makers on its payroll, and can legitimately claim to have kept alive the Grierson flame. By comparison with many independently produced documentaries, however, many of its products are somewhat staid. Canadians have enriched world culture by leaving Canada, working in the United States or elsewhere. The same cannot be said of Canadian documentaries. In Australia, a similar addiction to cultural protectionism has produced much the same result – conservative films with Australian themes.

68   The decades-long changes in public broadcasting are outside the scope of this publication. But they can be tracked through the fortunes of documentaries. Documentaries, once widely considered to be 'the DNA of public broadcasters', in the phrase of Brian Winston, shown in peak time, have become canaries in the mineshaft. Television has striven to connect itself with easily defined audiences, but these have increasingly consisted of older people. The educative function of television has been partly abandoned in favour of entertainment.

Some film boards do avoid the trap of regionalism. Among them is the Irish Film Board, which interprets Irish subjects very loosely. In a short time, with modest funds, the Irish Film Board has sponsored a variety of interesting projects. With similar goals, Britain's Film Council was not entirely successful. Compared with its over-ambitious commitment to propping up the British film industry, documentaries were always an unimportant part of its activities. It was obliged to consider the commercial viability of documentaries. In practice, this led to the support of mostly safe projects. Many of these were not successful in cinemas. The Film Council's most successful project was *Man on Wire* (2008), a co-production with the BBC which won the 2009 Oscar. Would *Man on Wire* have been made without the Film Council? It probably would have been, but with greater difficulty. Following the abolition of the Film Council by the new coalition government in 2010, the task of sponsoring documentaries has been returned to the British Film Institute (BFI). But it is not yet clear what criteria they are supposed to employ. Do they fund the sort of arthouse fare neglected by the BBC and Channel Four? Or do they work with the BBC and Channel Four? They will probably try to do both, all the while retaining some of the commercial obligations espoused by the Film Council.

The most successful non-broadcast funding sources tend to have existed for some time, developing their distinctive cultures. The Independent Television Service (ITVS) was set up in the US in 1990, after film-makers had run a campaign complaining about the excess bureaucracy of PBS, the Public Broadcasting System. ITVS is funded by public television. It is based in liberal San Francisco, and since 2005 has also run an international programme. With limited resources it remains one of the most effective sources of funding in the US, entering into partnerships with foundations, and filling gaps in budgets with the help of non-American broadcasters. Panels selecting projects for ITVS are made up of practitioners. There is a degree of leftish conservatism in the choices, which seems inevitable given the location of ITVS. By and large, however, the choices are sound and often adventurous.

The Danish Film Institute (DFI) was created in 1972, and apart from the feature films it supports each year it invests in up to 30 documentaries each year, with a total budget of £5.5 million (50 million kroner). The DFI interprets its obligations to support Danish film culture liberally. It accepts films made in the English language, and has supported international ventures, even when the directors or producers are not Danish, if the projects are considered to be in the Danish interest. (A radical aspect of the institute is the insistence that those who choose projects shouldn't stay longer than a few years, thus in principle assuring perpetually fresh eyes.) Most projects backed by the DFI find their way onto one or other of the Danish television networks but this isn't mandated.

The premises of the DFI are above a cultural complex, and the institute is run by a former newspaper executive, Henrik Bo Nielsen. He explains that in the past ten years the institute has shifted its interest in two ways. It no longer nurses the fantasy that documentaries can exist outside television. When I ask him how films are chosen, he explains that there can never be a single criterion. 'We know when we have failed,' he said, 'because no one is interested in the film.' They were helped by younger film-makers, who no longer wanted to make films that never found audiences. 'Danish success with films has become important to us,' he suggested. 'If you are a Dane who wants to make an impact on the world, nowadays you make films. And among the best Danish films are documentaries.'

But the film fund culture is a province of the old, social democratic tradition of public provision, now weakened by the cult of the market, and threatened in the same way as the BBC. Elsewhere shrinking budgets are pushing film-makers towards new sources of funding. In the US foundations have long proved to be the mainstay of funding for PBS, since the creation of the public network in the 1960s, and they have become more important. There are, to be sure, right-wing foundations with an interest in media. By and large, however, they do not put money into films.[69] So the field has been left to organisations such as the Ford Foundation, which recently earmarked $50 million for documentaries, and George Soros's constellation of organisations grouped around the ideas of the Open Society Institute. Between 1996 and 2008 the OSI spent at least $5.2 million helping to create several hundred documentaries. All of these organisations share a similar, mildly liberal interest in social activism.

At first sight the array of liberal institutions united around the promotion of a better world is impressive. One may indeed feel what a radical would have experienced in 1930s New York, surrounded by so many small-scale left-leaning publications dedicated to social change. But there is a price to be paid, notoriously, even for the best intentions. One can sign up to these goals, and still experience reservations about the direction implied by such powerful influences. In a Manhattan hotel I sat down one afternoon in 2006 with Jeff Skoll, founder of E-bay, and representative of the new breed.[70] Skoll

69   The question of why the cultural right has so little interest in funding non-fiction films is an intriguing one. No slouch when it comes to polemics, the American right has failed to fund even one proficient documentary film. (They are also adept when it comes to discouraging film-makers seeking to infiltrate their ranks.) This may be because American film-makers are drawn from the ranks of the liberal left. But it also may reflect some deep-rooted indifference towards the mixture of observation and bias that characterises many political documentaries. The American right tends to run on anger, whereas indignation is the stock-in-trade of documentary film. This means that Michael Moore makes films whereas Glenn Beck, Rush Limbaugh, Ann Coulter, Sarah Palin et al. appear before cameras, ranting. There again, as cynics observe, why make a film when you can own or guarantee unlimited appearance on a television channel?

70   Author's interview, New York 2006. Skoll's company Participant Media spells out its ambitious world-changing aims in an online mission statement: 'The company seeks to entertain audiences first, then to invite them to participate in making a difference. To facilitate this, Participant creates specific social action campaigns for each film and documentary designed to give a voice to issues that resonate in the films' (participantmedia.com).

was well dressed, mild in appearance, earnest in the best Canadian way. His foundation and his company invested in fiction and documentaries – he didn't really differentiate between the two – and he organised social action programmes around his films. In the style of a business school presentation he explained how things should work. 'You should never undertake too much,' he explained patiently. 'It's better to have more impact with one film than waste time with too many outlets.'

Would Skoll's energies ever be deployed in favour of public interests that didn't coincide with his own? What would be his attitude to films that argued the case for changing the world, but couldn't be linked to public campaigns? This wasn't clear. Meanwhile it was clear that Skoll saw films as tools in a larger undertaking, that of remodelling society. Skoll's dream has indeed been realised, and not just in his own films. Agitprop has become fashionable again, and there are private individuals, companies, and foundations eager to invest in films that claim to save civilisation. These films are more fluent than the old-style heavily instructional ones of the last century. They aim to seduce while instructing. They are not 'balanced', lacking even the pretence of equipoise claimed by their antecedents. But they are also, taken as a whole, somewhat predictable. As Arthur Koestler meanly remarked about liberals, when they start a sentence, you know how it will end. When you enter such a film, you know where you will be taken.

One argument in favour of such work, frequently rehearsed in the US, is that the mainstream media are so biased to the right that it can do no harm to see films tilted in the opposite direction. It is possible to acknowledge this, admiring the public-spiritedness of people like Skoll, and still experience a degree of misgiving. What has happened to the old, capacious notion that you don't have to tell people what to think, indeed that showing them things is a better idea? Everywhere in journalism the old tradition of impartiality is under assault. In the view represented by Skoll and others, documentary films are no longer wholly attached to journalism. They exist somewhere in a separate realm, between self-improvement and liberal propaganda. They are there to make us better people. In a world getting daily more hazardous, it is suggested, we have no alternative but to submit to a regime of self-improvement.

And yet it would be wrong to dismiss this tendency, not least because the task of reclaiming journalism from extinction is so huge. Maybe we will never see again so much objectivity deployed daily in search of relevant facts. And maybe much of the old journalistic tradition wasn't so very glorious, or indeed very objective. Skoll has put money into the task of attempting to reclaim what remains of local journalism in the US from the depredations of the internet. He has made sure that many subjects, which would otherwise have gone unaired, have reached audiences. In 2011 he contributed funds to ensure the showing of *Page One*, a film which described a year in the life of the *New York Times* from the perspective of David Carr, its media columnist, an ex-crack addict and single parent with a cult following among media geeks. Doleful, with the air of an abbot of a failing monastery, Carr was faithful to the tradition of impartiality of the old *Times* journalism, striving to uphold it. As the *Times* lost money, cutting back on its staffing levels, he appeared to be fighting a losing battle. Among many detailed scenes was the account of how the *Chicago Tribune*, once a good paper, had fallen into the hands of radio marketing men, going bankrupt shortly after trivialising itself. But this wasn't a gloomy story. Carr didn't despair of the future, and nor, it seemed, did the many hard-working *Times* people. They believed that their own style of reporting would somehow survive the flood. Here was an unexpected gift: an unstrident, thoughtful film campaigning in favour of careful, dispassionate journalism, financed by a campaigner. Skoll, significantly, wasn't telling us how he or anyone else could restore the fortunes of reporting. That would be left to the *New York Times*.

Several times a year, in the US, the UK, and now in Europe, it is possible to attend gatherings of the Good Pitch. This is organised by the Britdoc Foundation,[71] which is paid for by Channel Four, with support from the Sundance Institute. No suggestion of commerce pervades these proceedings. Broadcasters are by and large confined to the audience, and pitches are now made to representatives of foundations, NGOs, and new funds that subscribe to the idea of promoting 'social action' through film.[72] There tends to be no discussion of how a film will look, or indeed how and why it will please an audience. Nor is there a sense that messages should be nuanced or part hidden, or indeed whether it's a good idea for films to be sent out carrying such unequivocally expressed messages. Instead, the focus is on what are strictly organisational, practical matters. After the validity of the project is acknowledged – the degree to which it subscribes to approved social goals – 'partnering' is discussed. If enough partners are assembled, the idea is that a message can gain mass. People will agree with a film, and their lives will be changed. By dint of repetition, or freely expressed conviction, the world will be changed. Is it possible to imagine a future in which documentaries, spun off from their mixed inheritance of journalism and entertainment, do in fact alter the world? Along with many others, the people at the Good Pitch seem

71   The Britdoc Foundation was created in 2005, and it gives money for the development and production of documentaries, up to £30,000. Although paid for by Channel Four, it is independent of the channel, making its own choices. Channel Four has first option on Britdoc films and, for a small additional contribution, can acquire the right to show them, though it has latterly declined to do so, preferring more commercial films set in less remote parts of the world and without subtitles. To date Britdoc has part-funded over 60 award-winning films. The Good Pitch is a recent addition to the foundation's activities.

72   Among them is Pumavision, from the sports goods manufacturer Puma, which has sponsored a prize of £35,000 annually for the best documentary on a social action theme. The Bertha Foundation has donated the money for two years for two separate funds, one for investigative reporting, the other for 'outreach' – i.e. giving a documentary a life subsequent or alternative to the one it enjoys on television.

to be saying yes.

Another interesting innovation is 'crowd funding' – the use of many individual contributors. Go to kickstart.com and you'll find projects in search of investors. Search online for the work of Alan Greenwald. At least five of his documentaries on subjects such as Walmart or Fox News have been funded in this way. At the other extreme, consider the fate of *My Reincarnation*, a film about a father and son, both Buddhists, painstakingly made by the New York film-maker Jennifer Fox. With a shortfall of $50,000 she organised a fund-raising campaign in tandem with showings of the film, appealing to those interested in the film to contribute more than they would by merely buying a ticket. Through the website Kickstarter Fox has already raised $150,000.

These strategies may be useful, but to this date they remain marginal. They don't address the question of how documentaries can be adequately funded, because, even taken together, they do not supply a replacement for the old system of funding documentaries, which is television. The truth is that documentaries are threatened most of all by the decline of funds and interest in broadcast television.[73] Usually crises are deemed to exist when they display many external signs, or when it is clear that some half-trusted way of doing things is about to collapse. No such emergency signs surround the funding and production of documentaries. But the situation is worrying enough. Are documentaries a threatened species? 'We know the money is hard to find,' Simon Kilmurry, editor of the PBS series *POV*, explains. 'But the harder it becomes the more we show, and the more we rely on them.' Only the BBC, NHK in Japan, or HBO still can afford the luxury of paying for their own product, and it would seem likely that BBC cuts, requiring a reduction of 20% over five years, will shortly end the latter's privileged position.

---

73   Recently, Channel Four abandoned its policy of regularly showing documentaries from all over the world in the *True Stories* strand on its digital channel More Four. Instead it will programme ten more popular titles (i.e. in English, or without subtitles, focused on tabloid subjects), funding these titles better. In the short term this is a gain for cash-strapped film-makers, but it is yet another instance of shrinking possibilities.

6.   Conclusion and Recommendations

If the traditional sources of funding are drying up, how will documentaries survive? Will they be altered by the new methods of distribution afforded online? Will it shortly be redundant to speak of documentary films, as they become just another part of the agglomeration of images, sounds, and words known as media? Tim Wu's book, *The Master Switch* (2010), convincingly describes a series of media empires in the 20th century, each of them cataclysmically displaced by what the Austrian economist Joseph Schumpeter called 'creative destruction'. It is possible to resist these changes, Wu suggests, but only if one is prepared to rig the regulatory framework. Corporations which have acquired a dominant place in the market do so regularly, but their efforts are ultimately overwhelmed. It would seem that we are in the midst of a new upheaval, and Wu argues that we must do all we can to preserve the internet's 'uniquely open design', with its revolutionary implications, from the depredations of monopolists.

In this respect, he is surely correct. Viewed from another perspective, that of documentaries, the argument for an open internet is overwhelming. Too much has been written about the power of the internet to change the form in which we acquire information. The 'objective' style of news reporting pioneered by modern newspapers at the end of the 19th century survived its importation into radio and television. It has been weakened by the sheer volume of polemic available on the internet, and by such innovations as Fox News. But it still commands loyalty among readers or viewers, and there can be no suggestion that the perceived need for such qualities will disappear because of the internet. (It may be altered as a consequence of the interests dominating the internet, but that is a different matter.) On a smaller scale, despite the up-and-down past, the same can be said about documentaries. Many people take the view that documentaries will always survive – because there will always be enough young people willing to make them for nothing. This is the view of the television critic A. A. Gill, for instance. 'I can't see that it matters if you only make one documentary in your life,' he says. 'The point is that it should be a good one.'[74] Others such as Errol Morris are inured to the vagaries of funding, and are able either to do other things in order to make a living (in Errol's case shooting commercials) or well-off enough to be able to subsidise their own work. My own view lies somewhere between such views and the expectation that, against the odds, there will be institutions in the future capable of lavishly funding them. If documentaries are a public good, in the same way as reporting, as I believe they are, they should be recognised as such. But their distinctive history, and the erratic, idiosyncratic means of financing hitherto applied, means that no single solution can be applied to them.

Things which resemble documentaries will survive, but they will only flourish if we manage to think in a different way about their prospects. No radical recasting is required in my view, merely what social psychologists call a 'nudge' to the various players. The assumption must be that, while television will merge with the internet as it becomes easier to view what you want when you want, nonetheless television will remain a force governing the content of news and documentaries, at least for the next decade. And within that context documentaries will continue to evolve as they have done, shedding some outdated characteristics, but remaining a means among others of making sense of the world.

The best documentaries are independent. They don't exist to serve interests, philanthropic or otherwise. Like the best journalism, like films for that matter, they represent the vision of the world of their directors, producers, or reporters. The past years have shown how much talent can be found, all over the world. All we need to do is find the talent, and find a way of bringing it to other people. It is the latter which is changing so rapidly, but this need not be to the disadvantage of documentaries.

Here, therefore, are some recommendations. These are simple measures, and, if implemented, they would make it easier to sustain ambitious documentaries.

Television

Documentaries are an inexpensive, vital part of public television. Television should get to love them more instead of consigning them to poor slots, as an afterthought.

Television appears to have abandoned the idea that it can occasionally speak for all people, and not merely inhabit the niche demographics beloved of market researchers. It isn't hard to collaborate with radio stations, newspapers, and the internet. If audiences are falling in public television, maybe television executives need to take more risks. At its founding in 1981, Channel Four's Charter obliged it to 'demonstrate innovation, experiment and creativity in

---

74   In conversation with the author.

the form and content of programmes'. The same injunction must be placed on public broadcasters with respect to factual programming, and it needn't lead broadcasters to regard the obligation as a burden, requiring the presence of dull films. If necessary the obligation to make sense of the world by showing documentaries should be incorporated into the parliamentary statutes licensing broadcasters – with the obligation that they should be shown at a time when people can watch them, and also on the internet.

The boldest showcasing of documentaries has been in Scandinavia, where both SVT in Sweden and DR in Denmark have recently created once-a-week, middle-of-the-evening documentary slots, marketing them aggressively. In both cases the experiments have been successful.[75] There are also new ways in which broadcasters can work together. Among these are the ventures organised around STEPS, a small foundation based in Cape Town.[76] When the scale of the AIDS epidemic in Southern Africa became apparent, over 30 broadcasters clubbed together to supply funds and expertise, making possible a substantial series of full-length films and shorts from local film-makers. These were shown throughout the region (they were first aired on television, but were later distributed via mobile cinemas in townships, accompanied by talks and educative material) and, later, broadcast throughout the West.

A subsequent project, Why Democracy?, assembled a similar number of broadcasters globally willing to show ten full-length films on the theme of the progress, or non-progress, of global democracy.[77] Another project, Why Poverty?, is currently in production, and it will be aired in November 2012. This time the online component of the mix is substantially more ambitious, enlarging the scope of the films and making the investment in such an ambitious project capable of yielding much larger returns.

How do you make people aware of what you are doing? How do you win them over, not just to the worth of a certain argument, but to the fact that such an argument exists at all? How do you educate the world? Such efforts aren't isolated, and there will presumably be more of them. They seem important because they are ambitious, and they are making a stab at resolving the problem faced by anyone not just making documentary films, but engaged in any variety of public illumination or persuasion.

The most important recommendation for television is that its executives should once more cherish documentaries. If they don't, and television restricts

---

75   Documania at Damemarks Radio.

76   I've been involved in each of these ventures, and currently am chairman of STEPS International, a foundation independent of the Cape Town STEPS and based in Copenhagen.

77   The films were successful, winning many prizes, including an Oscar. Their success in individual countries and markets tended to be dependent on exactly how much effort each broadcaster put into the task of promoting them. In Sweden, for instance, the head of Swedish television went on the news each night for a week in order to tell people to watch the films. In Brazil, DVDs of the films, accompanied by educational material, were sent to 1,000 schools and community centres by Futura, an educational foundation, packed into a special democracy suitcase.

itself to factual formats, or takes refuge in parochial evocations of 'national' culture, documentaries on television will die. At the BBC most people would assent to the proposition that documentaries are important, and must be shown. But the documentary culture doesn't exist in many television stations. So here are two recommendations: first, so long as public television exists, it should be made to carry documentaries by regulatory authorities such as Ofcom, both at times when they can be readily seen, and online, as part of the archive; second, that television, acting through producers, should think internationally.

Voices

Consider what happens in print journalism. The views of owners obtrude fairly often into the priorities or coverage of newspapers. Defenders of the status quo in television point out that channels operate with a public licence, and that this confers the obligation to be impartial. There are two practical reasons why it should be modified in relation to documentaries. The first is that not all documentaries are, or should be, considered to be impartial. The second is that the existing rules fail to distinguish between overtly propagandistic sources of funding, and those that exist to supply money in order to get subjects talked about.

No one gives money away for no reason at all. Imagine that you have suddenly become very rich. It is understandable that you might want to contribute to the betterment of humanity. You may even want to save the world. You may want to promote the rights of hedgehogs, or bring to light the views of those who were abducted by aliens and lived to tell the tale. These will seem legitimate causes, and no one should stop you doing what you want. Should you be able to fund a film expressing these views? Of course. Should this film be shown on public television? In the past, public television has shied away from such prospects. But the presence of private money and private opinions in factual films causes more problems for broadcasters than it should do. The banning of overt or covert political messages in films is reasonable. It is also not true that such content is hard to spot. Graham Greene once said that he became aware of flaws in his plots in the same way as an expert came to know about dry rot. The same applies to political propaganda. But there are many forms of polemical expression short of outright propaganda. 'All art is propaganda,' Orwell wrote, and he meant to say that nothing, least of all news reporting, was 'pure'. That didn't mean that you shouldn't be exposed to propaganda, for you couldn't help that, and anyhow you would only know what to think once you had been.

Another recommendation: broadcasters no longer have the money or the inclination to fund factual projects in their entirety. They must distinguish more clearly now between the money they won't touch, and the kind of support they are prepared to allow. They can make space, selectively, for more campaigning films. They can tolerate more heterodox views. Broadcasters should also cease to be prim when it comes to collaboration with foundations that share their values.

And broadcasters are, whether they like it or not, liberal institutions. They were funded in order to uphold free speech, tolerance etc. They should be encouraging foundations to earmark money for educational purposes, rather than worrying about the implications. The argument that audiences, having paid through a licence fee or taxes for programmes, shouldn't be exposed to anything funded in a different way isn't sustainable – on practical grounds alone it misses the mark, but it also fails to address the sheer diversity of programmes available, which private people or organisations are willing to fund.

For their part, however, foundations should resist the temptation to give up on broadcasters. One of the most depressing aspects, if you work for a broadcaster, has been the evolution among those foundations of a hostile or dismissive view towards broadcasters. Snobbery is at the root of this, but frustration, too. One need not think of television as rubbish, even if many of those who work in television do sometimes act as if it were rubbish. The old-fashioned distinction between so-called 'art' documentaries, which are deemed worthy of special treatment, and the rest, which are not, ceased to have any basis in contemporary culture long ago.

Another recommendation: an interdiction, therefore, against preciousness. Film funds should no longer act in isolation, and they should abandon the notion of a privileged aesthetic or social sphere of documentaries. They should also give up on the idea of funding only documentaries capable of doing well in cinemas. Instead they should become part of the rough and tumble of getting attention for good films.

There are start-up funds and distribution funds. But money for production is hard to come by. And this is where film funds should be working – backing not just famous directors but promising ones. Both film funds and broadcasters should welcome the presence of private or corporate support for new projects. The only criterion that should be used in relation to such contributions indeed should be whether it supports the independence of the film-maker and whatever seems cogent or original in the film-maker's vision.

The internet

'The internet is like a permanent earthquake,' a top BBC executive remarked at a seminar in Oxford. 'From week to week we have to alter our estimates not of how it ends, because we have no idea, but where it is going next.' It has been suggested that the act of downloading favours short films. But this could be because longer ones until recently required reactivation every ten minutes or so. It may be that non-fiction films will simply become part of the hybrid post-tabloid blog-hit-and-run style of contemporary media. Mixtapes are what they will shortly be. More likely is that long documentaries will continue to exist alongside shorter ones – you can see this happening already in the readiness of film-makers to post shorter versions of their work on YouTube. But the longer versions are present, too – on YouTube channels as well as the BBC iPlayer.

The vogue for interesting long-form documentaries answers to some real desire. It doesn't seem unlikely that viewers will be prepared to pay to watch documentaries. And indeed documentaries are already being viewed in this way. Individual film-makers are making their own way online. How to distribute your own film? Ben Lewis explains that he now ships copies of his films from his flat: 'if people want your work they will find it,' he says. But Lewis thinks that film-makers are in a race for survival – against the odds they may find a way of making money from their own films before existing sources dry up. 'But I wouldn't bet on it,' he says. 'Many of the best film-makers are not inconsiderable businessmen. But they are trapped within the worst business model. That's their fate and their privilege – because penury means you have no choice but to remain independent.'[78]

Early efforts to enhance the performance of documentaries online consisted of sites filled with accompanying material, and the best of these convey the essence of a project long after it has been aired on television.[79] It soon became evident that such activity implied a limited vision of the potential of the internet. A more interesting indication of the future was supplied by the fact that one could judge the success of a new documentary by the time it took to pirate the film, putting it on YouTube. Rapidly, YouTube has become a repository of old documentaries, most of them shortened to six or ten minutes. Among its many other functions, it has become an informal archive of non-fiction film. But Google, which owns YouTube, has now created a series of channels. Companies or institutions can now post their own channels on YouTube, making whatever they wish available to a global audience via Google. And Google has now begun to fund content, including documentaries. Another pointer to the future came with the arrival of the BBC's iPlayer service, which makes television programmes available to viewers outside the broadcast schedules for a limited time. Among the surprise successes are documentaries.[80] The BBC iPlayer is now being made available globally. Some services will be paid for by subscribers, others may be free, in the old BBC tradition.

In fewer than ten years most of what is still known as broadcasting, or television, will have been engulfed by the internet. Will people watch

---

78   Interview with the author.
79   As a sample of these see WGBH's carefully constructed sites.
80   It wasn't unusual, for instance, for Storyville titles to show up second or third in the list of most viewed programmes, despite the fact that the films had appeared on a minority channel, BBC4.

programmes at all as they used to, in carefully constructed sequences? Will everything but the news, sports, and the odd royal wedding, be part of some vast archive? A guess would be that much of what is immediate – the mix of the topical and the out-of-time that characterises cable or network television in the US – will be available in the same way as now. Broadcast will be digital, but whatever is viewed in the form of a schedule will constitute a shop window for the larger online service of archive or subscription material. Documentaries will be viewed primarily on demand, at one's convenience, though some will still be found in schedules of diminished importance.

Already, docs are shown online. IDFA, the Amsterdam documentary festival, offers an archive of documentaries, and Finnish television allows you to scan some documentaries about the Afghan war. Last year France Télévision announced its intention of placing the entire archive of French television online. These are bold moves, to be sure, but not all of them reflect a real attempt to sound out the likely preferences of audiences. Instead of coming out of any real comprehension of the way in which media are likely to be utilised, many reflect a growing panic when it comes to the prospect of being left behind. Meanwhile the future is taking shape. It is now possible to charge online for a new documentary.[81] Netflix, which is based in Los Gatos, California, has hitherto shipped DVDs to its 25 million subscribers; but now the service will be available online. One can easily see a Netflix-style service maturing into a visual equivalent of Amazon's online service Kindle.[82] (Amazon, too, has plans to deliver films online.) But there are certainly other ways of showing documentaries on the internet, as yet unexplored.[83]

Here, however, are two interim recommendations. It would seem, first, that documentaries aren't as immediately threatened as print reporting by the existence of the internet – because they are funded and distributed in so many different ways, and because their makers have always had to contend with penury. But that is no reason not to encourage their migration. They should become part of the near limitless public space of the internet, with its vast educational possibilities. But they will also, surely, occupy a niche place in which producers (or the successors to broadcasters) can charge for premium viewers. So organisations such as the BBC should be encouraged to develop internet distribution immediately.

The capability of claiming and securing attention is the most elusive

81   *Shooting Robert King* (2001), a film about a young war photographer, was compiled from ten years of footage by the founders of London's Frontline Club, Vaughan Smith and Richard Parry. It didn't find favour with broadcasters, who thought that there had been many films on the subject. However, it was downloaded by 150,000 viewers.
82   For an optimistic, utopian view of the online prospects of Netflix see Brian Appleyard, *Sunday Times,* 1 Jan. 2012.
83   Software now exists enabling a film or book to be accessed via any number of totally different sites, while its owners collect cash from each viewing or sale.

commodity in contemporary media. It costs little to make material available on the internet, a lot to find ways of making sure people become aware that it is there. It is hard to imagine that many documentaries will be able to find global audiences without the active intervention of major players like the BBC. In ten years' time the huge network of services that go to make up the BBC World Service will have migrated online. So will the BBC's worldwide television service.

The BBC at the very least should step forward, playing its part, offering, perhaps with partners, a global online documentary service. Much of what is offered should be free, in line with the BBC's long-established mission to educate the world. But some of the material can be offered as part of a premium service, available on subscription or viewed for a fee. Why should the BBC (or another current factual brand such as CNN, or Al-Jazeera) bother to create such a service? Because this is how documentaries can be helped to make their way in the world. And because doing this will re-establish, in an internet context, the BBC's global educative mission. Because, ultimately, this is how the BBC will survive.

Freedoms

No cultural policy should be forever – because tastes change so rapidly. And it would be a mistake to enshrine documentaries as an object of patronage. They are really 'the brief abstract and chronicle of the time' – but no less valuable because of that. Ultimately anything should be permitted that encourages independent documentaries.

Documentaries remain interesting to us as a consequence of the state of freedom in which they and their makers exist. They should not become the exclusive property either of a lobby devoted to good intentions, or of a heavily subsidised system producing artefacts for display in the remaining arthouses. Nor should they be conscripted in the struggle to preserve national, regional or ethnic cultures. Documentaries are reliant on whatever happens, minute by minute. Documentaries are maybe most at risk because they rely so much on the contingent. More than texts written for performance, or films that rely on scripts, they exist as a consequence of impulse, easily destroyed by an excess of calculation and supervision.

We can't begin to know how such a state of freedom can be conserved. What we can do, however, is acknowledge how much documentaries, along with other forms of cultural expression, contribute to freedoms. In a small way, therefore, encouraging documentary film may become a way in which we come to think what it means to be bold, free and enquiring, seeing the world as it really is, and not in the way that others would want us to see it.

Appendix 1: Fifty Great Documentaries

All available on Amazon except those marked with an asterisk (*).

Dziga Vertov, *Man with a Movie Camera* (1929)

Humphrey Jennings, *The Complete Humphrey Jennings: Volume One* (1934–40)

Leni Riefenstahl, *Triumph of the Will* (1935)

Fred W. Friendly , Edward R. Murrow, *Edward R. Murrow: Joe McCarthy See it Now* (9 March 1954)

Alain Resnais, *Night and Fog* (1955)

Robert Drew, *Primary* (1960)

John Terraine, Corelli Barnett, *The Great War* (1964)

D. A. Pennebaker, *Don't Look Back* (1967)

Frederick Wiseman, *Titicut Follies* (1967)

Albert Maysles, David Maysles, Charlotte Zwerin, *Salesman* (1968)

Louis Malle, *Phantom India* (1969)

Marcel Ophüls, *The Sorrow and the Pity* (1969)

Albert Maysles, David Maysles, Charlotte Zwerin, *Gimme Shelter* (1970)

Hugh Raggett, John Pett, David Elstein, Ted Childs, Michael Darlow, Martin Smith, *The World at War* (1974)

Ellen Hovde, Albert Maysles, David Maysles, Muffie Meyer, *Grey Gardens* (1975)

Robin Anderson, Bob Connolly, *First Contact* (1982)

Claude Lanzmann, *Shoah* (1985)

Kazuo Hara, *The Emperor's Naked Army Marches On* (1987)

Henry Hampton, *Eyes on the Prize* (1987)

Marcel Ophüls, *Hotel Terminus* (1988)

Errol Morris, *The Thin Blue Line* (1988)

Ken Burns, *The Civil War* (1990)

Nick Broomfield, *The Leader, his Driver and the Driver's Wife* (1991)

Chris Hegedus, D. A. Pennebaker, *The War Room* (1993)

Terry Zwigoff, *Crumb* (1994)

Steve James, *Hoop Dreams* (1994)

Norma Percy, Angus Macqueen, Paul Mitchell, *The Death of Yugoslavia** (1995)

Leon Gast, *When We Were Kings* (1996)

Werner Herzog, *Little Dieter Needs to Fly* (1998)

Leslie Woodhead, *A Cry From the Grave** (1999)

Kevin Macdonald, *One Day in September* (1999)

Mark Lewis, *The Natural History of the Chicken* (2000)

José Padilha, Felipe Lecerda, *Bus 174* (2002)

Andrew Jarecki, *Capturing the Friedmans* (2003)

Nick Broomfield, Joan Churchill, *Aileen Wuornos: The Life and Death of a Serial Killer* (2003)

Nathaniel Kahn, *My Architect* (2003)

Kevin Macdonald, *Touching the Void* (2003)

Jehane Noujaim, *Control Room* (2004)

Hubert Sauper, *Darwin's Nightmare* (2004)

Jean-Xavier de Lestrade, *The Staircase* (2004)

Alex Gibney, *Enron: The Smartest Guys in the Room* (2005)

Werner Herzog, *Grizzly Man* (2005)

Robert Stone, *Guerrilla: The Taking of Patty Hearst* (2005)

Eugene Jarecki, *Why We Fight* (2005)

Spike Lee, *When the Levees Broke: A Requiem in Four Acts* (2006)

Weijun Chen, *Please Vote for Me* (2007)

Alex Gibney, *Taxi to the Dark Side* (2007)

Geoffrey Smith, *The English Surgeon* (2007)

James Marsh, *Man on Wire* (2008)

Janus Metz Pederson, *Armadillo* (2010)

Appendix 2: Box Office Successes

Table 1. Top 20 Documentaries at the UK Box Office, 2000–2009

	Title	Origin	Release	Box office gross (£)	Widest point of release (sites)	Distributor
1	Michael Jackson's This Is It	USA	2009	9,795,960	498	Sony Pictures
2	Fahrenheit 9/11	USA	2004	6,545,552	200	Optimum
3	March of the Penguins	France	2005	3,084,616	163	Warner Bros
4	Touching the Void	UK	2003	2,643,252	50	Pathé
5	Bowling for Columbine	USA	2002	1,667,625	37	Momentum
6	Super Size Me	USA	2004	1,111,093	83	Tartan
7	An Inconvenient Truth	USA	2006	935,770	68	Paramount
8	Man on Wire	UK/USA	2008	879,377	43	Icon
9	Hannah Montana/Miley Cyrus: Best of Both Worlds	USA	2008	799,109	65	Disney
10	U2 3D	USA	2008	725,893	67	Revolver
11	Être et Avoir	France	2003	708,116	15	Tartan
12	Shine a Light	USA/UK	2008	697,320	159	20th Century Fox
13	Spellbound	USA	2003	484,540	17	Metrodome
14	The September Issue	USA	2009	427,767	18	Momentum
15	Capturing the Friedmans	USA	2004	388,238	26	Tartan
16	Sicko	USA	2007	378,669	166	Optimum
17	The Corporation	Canada	2004	296,234	20	Metrodome
18	Jonas Brothers: The 3D Concert	USA	2009	249,534	169	Disney
19	Of Time and the City	UK	2008	245,189	25	BFI
20	Lost in La Mancha	UK/USA	2002	233,383	13	Optimum

Source: UK Film Council RSU analysis of Rentrak EDI data.

Note: The table does not include IMAX-only documentaries and shorts. Based on box office data for 2000–2009. *Michael Jackson's This Is It* is regarded as the highest grossing documentary of all time because, even with price inflation, it is unlikely that any documentary films before 1989 will have earned more in nominal terms.

Table 2. Top Grossing Documentaries at the US Box Office (IMAX Excluded)

Rank	Title	Studio	Lifetime Gross/Theatres		Opening/Theatres		Date
1	Fahrenheit 9/11	Lions	$119,194,771	2,011	$23,920,637	868	23 June 04
2	March of the Penguins	WIP	$77,437,223	2,506	$137,492	4	24 June 05
3	Justin Bieber: Never Say Never	Par.	$55,886,443	3,118	$29,514,054	3,105	11 Feb. 11
4	Earth (2009)	BV	$32,011,576	1,804	$8,825,760	1,804	22 Apr. 09
5	Sicko	LGF	$24,540,079	1,117	$68,969	1	22 June 07
6	An Inconvenient Truth	ParC	$24,146,161	587	$281,330	4	24 May 06
7	Bowling for Columbine	UA	$21,576,018	248	$209,148	8	11 Oct. 02
8	Oceans	BV	$19,422,319	1,232	$6,058,958	1,206	22 Apr. 10
9	Madonna: Truth or Dare	Mira.	$15,012,935	625	$543,250	51	10 May 91
10	Capitalism: A Love Story	Over.	$14,363,397	995	$231,964	4	23 Sept. 09

Bibliography

Aufterheide, Pat, *Documentary Film: A Very Short Introduction* (Oxford University Press, 2007).

Ballard, J. G., *The Day of Creation* (Victor Gollancz, 1987).

– *The Kindness of Strangers* (HarperCollins, 1991).

Bruzzi, Stella, *New Documentary* (Routledge 2006).

Ellis, John, *Documentary: Witness and Self-Revelation* (Routledge, 2012).

Fitzwalter, Ray, *The Dream that Died: The Rise and Fall of ITV* (Matador, 2008).

Forman, Denis, *Persona Granada* (André Deutsch, 1997).

Herzog, Werner, *Herzog on Herzog*, ed. Paul Cronin (Faber & Faber, 2002).

Jackson, Kevin, *Humphrey Jennings* (Picador, 2004).

Lanzmann, Claude, *The Patagonian Hare* (Atlantic Books, 2012).

Macdonald, Kevin, and Cousins, Mark, *Imagining Reality: The Faber Book of Documentary* (Faber & Faber, 2006).

Malle, Louis, *Malle on Malle*, ed. Philp French (Faber & Faber 1993).

Seaton, Jean, *Carnage and the Media: The Making and Breaking of News about Violence* (Penguin, 2005).

Sperber, A. M., *Murrow: His Life and Times* (Freundlich Books, 1986).

Wood, Jason, *Nick Broomfield: Documenting Icons* (Faber & Faber 2005).

Wu, Tim, *The Master Switch* (Knopf, 2010).